CPR

for your

Sex Life

How to Breathe Life into
a Dead, Dying or Dull Sex Life

A Guide and Workbook for Couples

Mildred L. Brown, Ph.D.
Stephen L. Braveman, M.A.

To order additional copies, please contact:

BookSurge, LLC.
www.booksurge.com
1-866-308-6235

Acknowledgements

This book did not get to its completed form without the help of many individuals. We would like to thank Jeannette Cezanne, Nina Amir, Emily Friedman and Tammy Cravit for their part in editing this book and for all the suggestions and feedback that they gave us to help improve our book.

And, a very special thanks to Michaela Braveman, who spent many frustrating and hard-working hours formatting this book. She "saved" us several times.

We'd also like to thank our Booksurge team for their assistance and patience in pulling us through our book's final stages.

We are also appreciative of our many fellow therapists and colleagues who took the time to read our manuscript and give us their helpful comments and support.

And of course, we are especially grateful for our partners, Bernie and Michaela, and for our family and friends, who believed in us and stood by us, with love and saint-like patience, during the grueling and anxiety-filled months that it took us to complete this project. They kept us going emotionally on days when we were ready to give up.

And finally, we would like to thank the thousands of clients that we have worked with over the course of the past 30 years. They taught us what kind of sexual and relationship issues challenge couples enough to bring them into a therapist's office. Through them, we learned which interventions worked best to revive a relationship, and we have incorporated the resultant information into our book. This book is dedicated to them.

Contents

C
P
R

Conclusion

References

About the Authors

Introduction

C

P

R

The CPR Concept

Is your sex life dull, dying or dead even though you and your partner love each other?

If so, you are not alone. Over half of all couples in America struggle with this very common problem. In our over-scheduled and over-worked culture, many couples report feeling too tired for sex. In over 70% of two-parent households, both parents work outside the home. With ever more demands on us – childrearing, aging parents, health issues and financial struggles – finding the time and energy for a vital sex life is harder than ever before.

Furthermore, a couple's sex life can also deteriorate if one or both partners do not make sex a priority over their other activities. Many people spend so much time and energy engaging in hobbies, sports, exercise, the Internet and socializing that they are too tired and too distracted to devote time to their partner and to quality lovemaking.

A false belief that a deteriorating sex life is to be expected in a long-term relationship may have led many of you to feel hopeless and give up trying. The good news is that your situation is not hopeless. There is help. Your sex life can be revived and improved by working with this book.

When you first saw this book, you may well have wondered: What? Another book on sex? Why read this one, when we've already read several others – and are still unhappy? What can this book possibly offer that none of the others have?

As sex therapists who have worked with thousands of clients, we have found that most people forget the tools they've picked up from self-help books within a few weeks of reading them because many of these books are large and complex, and feel overwhelming and daunting to readers – certainly not feelings that help people to remember.

This book takes a different approach. It uses a short and simple format that will leave you with easily remembered suggestions to enhance your relationship and sex life, and will allow for easy review long after your first time through. How do we do this? Through something we call the "CPR" approach.

When most people hear the term CPR, the first thing that comes to mind is a medical, life-saving technique. Medical CPR is an emergency procedure performed when a person's breathing or heartbeat has stopped. CPR provides oxygen to the lungs and keeps oxygenated blood circulating until breathing and an effective heartbeat can be restored.

So why do we use the medical term CPR when referring to a couple's sexual relationship? The answer is simple: our society has bestowed "life" to the most intimate areas of our lives – social relationships and sex. We rarely ask "how is your work life?" or "how is your school life?" We ask "how's work?" or "how's school?" But for relationships and sex, we say "how's your social life?" or "how's your sex life?"

It is not surprising, therefore, that many of our clients use life and death terms when referring to sex. It is typical for a couple to come into our office and tell us, "our sex life has died (or is dying)," or "our sexual relationship has no energy; it's lifeless." Our typical response is to say, "we'll have to work on reviving it, or breathing some life back into your sexual relationship." Over time, we realized that what we and other sex therapists were doing in situations like this was sexual CPR – resuscitating an inert sex life until it was vital and alive again.

Medical *C P R*	Sexual *C P R*
Cardiac	**C**ouple
Pulmonary	**P**assion
Resuscitation	**R**esuscitation

Quite obviously, there are significant differences between medical CPR and sexual CPR:

- In medical CPR you are passive. Someone has to free your tongue, pound your chest and breathe life back into you. In sexual CPR, you must be an active participant. No outsider can revive your sex life for you. It takes the cooperation of both partners and the commitment to actively do whatever it takes to improve the situation.

- In medical CPR, time is of the essence – or you will die. In sexual CPR, you can take as long as you want to go through the program. In fact, taking time will improve the outcome.

- Medical CPR is structured. There are specific steps to perform in an exact order. In sexual CPR there are countless ways to revive your sex life, and they may be performed in a random order.

- Medical CPR requires no change by the patient to save their life. Sexual CPR requires change – what you have been doing doesn't work or you would not be seeking CPR.

Change is well worth the effort. When your passion and sex life are resuscitated, your self-esteem will skyrocket. You will feel more alive and enthusiastic. As sex therapists, we see that people actually live longer and have fewer ailments when they are sexually happy.

How to use this Book

This book is intended for couples who love each other but whose sex life is dull, dying or dead. In it, we present you with over 100 proven tools to use to enhance your relationship. At first glance, many of these tools and suggestions may seem to have nothing to do with sex, but we can assure you that they do. As you read through this book, you will see how they connect directly with sexual activity.

This will especially be true in long-term relationships where there is much more involved in romantic passion than simply dating and sex. Day-to-day interactions lay the foundation for either a poor or healthy sex life. What goes on in the kitchen and living room has a profound effect on what happens in the bedroom. When your partner treats you with respect and caring on a regular basis, you feel good about them and are more likely to be interested in them sexually.

If you have been having dissatisfying or infrequent sex, confusion, discomfort, resentment and even fear may have built up in you and your partner where sex is concerned. So it's futile to begin your CPR program with sexual activities. In order to move beyond your negative emotions, you need the slow buildup to sex that the CPR program provides.

The simple format we're using is to introduce a topic (which for your ease begins *only* with the letters C, P or R), speak of how it detracts from – or adds to – a couple's relationship or sex life, and then introduce our suggested solutions (called CPRs: Couple Passion Resuscitation exercises). Many of these CPRs will also walk you through a brief writing assignment.

It may seem to you that certain themes (such as appreciating the positive aspects of your relationship or complimenting your partner) are repeated throughout the book, sometimes in different ways. This is intentional. These are the themes that are vital in every aspect of the CPR process and will ultimately lead to a better sex life.

The topics in chapters two through five are presented in an alphabetical order, rather than in order of importance, as we believe that all the topics discussed are important ingredients for a good sex life. We don't want to presume to know which ones will be more meaningful for you. For optimal results, however, read everything and try all of the CPR suggestions. Take your time. Repeat each assignment as many times as you need in order to feel comfortable. Afterward, add some of your own ideas to build on the CPR suggestions and make them your own.

You will notice that the more sexually explicit suggestions come toward the end of the book in the "Advanced CPR" chapter. We strongly recommend that you wait to do those CPRs until you have completed all the prior ones. Emotional intimacy and sensuality are stepping-stones to a good sex life. Much of the book, therefore, is focused on building up couple intimacy as necessary groundwork for a healthy and satisfying sex life. We want you to strengthen these areas of your relationship first, before attempting the more sexual CPRs.

This book can be read alone or with your partner. Although one of the partners in the relationship can get suggestions from this book and use them to spice up the couple's sex life, best results are achieved when both partners read the book and make a commitment to devote time and attention to resuscitating their passion and their sex life. While you work together on the CPRs, remember that consistency is vital to the process, so make sure you follow through on everything you start. Also do each CPR several times at least. Doing something once does not produce a comfort level with it, nor does it show your partner your full involvement in the program. By being consistent you will build trust and let your partner know that you are wholly committed to your relationship.

While this is a workbook with space provided for you to write in, you will note that we have only provided writing space for one reader. If you are approaching this program correctly, however, there are two participants. One of you will need to keep a separate notebook. If you both prefer to keep this book free of writing, you may both use notebooks or store the information on a computer instead.

Some clients do the writing assignments grudgingly. They would prefer that we provide them with all the solutions to their problems. But, it is impossible for us to do that since every couple is made up of unique individuals with a unique set of issues. There is not one magical solution that works for everyone. Each couple needs to uncover what works best for them. The workbook format allows for a personalized exploration. The CPR exercises encourage and assist the readers to investigate their own emotional and sexual wants, turnons, turnoffs, and anxieties, and then deal with them through with the CPR tools presented in this book.

Please be aware that when we suggest that you write three things about a given topic, that it is not compulsory to come up with three. These numbers are only guidelines. You may write as many or as few items as are meaningful to you. Just make sure that you've really given thought to the issue.

If you want to hold onto the gain you've made from reading this book, revisit the book periodically after you complete your CPR program. Either reread the entire book or feel free to jump around as needed, and pick and chose the suggestions that you found most helpful to you and in your relationship.

Your age and physical health will determine whether you can recover the sex life that you once had. For example, if you were 45 years old when your sex life seemed to end, and you are now 74 years old, your physical abilities will be different. For men, it will most likely take you longer to obtain an erection and ejaculate. Women may need to supplement their own natural lubrication, and orgasms may be shorter and less intense. It may require effort and patience, but we can assure you that if you both want a recharged sex life, you can create one. It may look different than the one you had before, and it may not entirely match your fantasy of what it could be, but you will certainly have a more satisfying sex life than you do now.

We wish you good luck and good sex!

CHAPTER 1

| C |
| P |
| R |

C P R Essentials

In this part of the book, you'll learn six essential skills that you'll rely on when revitalizing and reinvigorating your sex life. Just as a house cannot be built without a solid foundation, it's not possible to revive a dying sex life without learning a few critical basic skills and tools. Once you've mastered these tools, you'll be ready to move on to the more complex techniques and skills that can breathe new life into your sex life.

Ready? Good. Let's begin.

CHECKUP

CHECKLIST   COMMUNICATION

COMMITMENT   CHANGE   COITUS (INTERCOURSE)

CHECKUP

When your physical health is failing, you make an appointment with a physician for a checkup, diagnosis, and hopefully for relief or a cure.

Imagine a situation where you make an appointment with your physician because you are not feeling well. You are not in pain, but you are tired. You don't have the energy that you once had and your mood is different. You have lost your enthusiasm.

Your physician will, of course, insist on a full checkup, including a physical exam and blood work. Before ordering tests, initiating treatment or writing a prescription, however, he or she does a full history to try to pinpoint what your problem is.

We too take a history and ask lots of probing questions of the people who come to see us for sex therapy. Until we've identified clearly what the problems are, it's difficult to decide which solutions stand the best chance of being successful.

Doing your own sex life checkup, therefore, is the first necessary step on your CPR path. Even though both you and your partner are committed to working on this CPR program, it is preferable that you each first do your own checkup. Take as much time as you need to do it. The more thorough the investigation, the more you will understand the surrounding circumstances of your sexual issues and be able to tailor a CPR routine that will be successful.

C P R:

Checkup – Part 1:

Perform your own sex life checkup. Answer the questions below:

1. What do you hope to gain by working with this book? What are your goals?

_____

_____

2. What is/are the sex problem(s) you are experiencing?

_____

_____

3. What symptoms did you first notice?

_____

_____

4. Under what circumstances did you notice them?

_____

_____

C

P

R

5. How long have these symptoms been present?

_____

_____

6. Do they come and go, or are they always there?

_____

_____

7. Do they interfere with your usual daily functioning? If so, how?

_____

_____

8. What do you think caused the current problem(s)?

_____

_____

9. Did something new or unusual occur in your life just before you first noticed your problem(s) (for example, a new job, a move, a new baby, health issues or new medication)?

_____

_____

10. *What have you done to try to remedy the situation?*

_____

_____

11. *Why do you think your attempted remedies did not work?*

_____

_____

12. *What do you think would work for you that you have not yet tried?*

_____

_____

13. *Are you struggling with any of the following: drug and/or alcohol dependence, domestic violence, abuse, an intrusive extended family or a rigid religious belief system?*

_____

_____

The issues in question 13 are beyond the scope of this book. If any of them are greatly impacting your life, we recommend that you seek professional mental health treatment prior to working with this book. This will ensure optimal success in your CPR program. You may also need a medical checkup to rule out an unrecognized, underlying disease.

Checkup – Part 2:

Some of you may have gotten new insights regarding your sex life from doing the checkup. Others of you may still be confused. It sometimes helps to look at the same issues from a different perspective so that new solutions may appear. Therefore, try examining your feelings using the CPR format below and see if you come up with new answers or added clarity to the previous questions.

CURRENT:

What is the current status of your sexual relationship? ("We have sex one time a month, it lacks passion and it's rushed," for example.)

_____

_____

PAST:

How was sex in the past? What was your best experience? What are you trying to restore? ("We used to have sex three times a week, with lots of foreplay and snuggling and pillow-talk afterward. I want that back," for example.)

_____

_____

RECIPE:

In medical CPR, when a patient is not breathing, there are clear-cut steps to follow – a recipe for saving their life. In sexual CPR, there are a multitude of recipes to save a sex life. For many, the recipe is stated in the form of an "if only" statement.

For example, the following statements are from our former clients' lists:

- *"If only I (or my partner) lost 20 pounds…*

- *"If only my partner would wear sexy lingerie to bed…*

- *"If only we had more privacy…*

- *"If only my partner were more romantic…*

…then we would have a good sex life."

Now list your "if only" statements:

_____

_____

_____

_____

_____

Checklist

The next step is to create a list of what you hope to gain from working with this book. Such a list will paint a picture of what you would like to see in your ideal sexual relationship, and help you understand what is missing.

Below are the lists of a mythical couple, we'll call Jack and Jill, indicating what they were hoping would come from working with this CPR book.

JILL'S LIST

I'd like him to:

- call me pet names
- do 10 minutes of touching each night
- help around the house
- call me during the day
- listen to me
- not push me to do certain things
- cuddle outside the bed
- compliment my appearance

JACK'S LIST

I'd like her to:

- greet me lovingly after work
- be nice to my friends
- kiss me several times a day
- show an interest in my hobbies
- lose 20 pounds
- initiate more often
- respect my after-work alone time
- meet me for lunch at work

As you see, Jill and Jack have very different lists, and each one of them may be unaware of what the other has been silently wishing for all this time! Just bringing it up and out into the open is a helpful first step in resolving communications problems around intimacy and sex.

C P R:

Start by making a list of at least five things that you want from your partner: things that would make you feel loved, appreciated and wanted, and that would help you look forward to sex.

1. _____

2. _____

3. _____

4. _____

5. _____

Next ask yourselves:

Which are the items on my list that exist in my life right now? One? All of them? None of them?

_____

_____

How many are "must haves" in order for you to enjoy sex?

_____

_____

Now go back to your list and number it in order of priority. Using Jack's and Jill's checklists below as models, make your own condensed weekly checklist from three to five of the "must haves" and "wants" on your list.

Take a look at Jack's and Jill's checklists below.

JILL'S CHECKLIST	MO	TUE	WED	THU	FR	SAT	SUN
5 minutes' touching							
Helps around the house							
Calls me pet names							
Compliments the way I look							

JACK'S CHECKLIST	MO	TUE	WED	THU	FR	SAT	SUN
Meets me for lunch at work							
Kisses me							
Shows an interest in my hobbies							
Greets me lovingly after work							

How did you do? Were you consciously aware of your wants and "must haves" before doing your checkup and making your list or did you just experience unexplainable discontent until now? If you weren't fully aware of what you wanted or needed in order to feel loved and look forward to sex, your can bet that your partner certainly wasn't aware of these things either. So, now that you've both made checklists, share them with each other and communicate in detail what it that you want.

Agree together to do your best to satisfy your partner's wants. If you can't accept an item on your partner's list, discuss it and see if they will replace it with one that you feel you can try. Post the checklist in a visible place, such as the bedroom mirror, and each night before going to sleep, make a check for each item on your partner's list that you believe you have completed. Your partner will do the same on your list.

Don't make a check unless your partner confirms the result. While you might not be able to complete each item every day, keep in mind that doing at least one thing for each other helps each of you feel special and provides you both with a sense of accomplishment.

At the end of the week sit down together and review the checklist. Give each other credit for those things that were accomplished and let each other know how good it feels to get the things you want from the person you love. Renegotiate any items that need it and create your list for the next week. As you see the progress, keep in mind that this is a useful tool throughout your relationship, not just for when you're having difficulties.

C

P

R

COMMUNICATION

Communication is a key part of every relationship and is vital to the success of your sexual relationship. Yet even some of the best communicators find it extremely difficult to talk about sex in general terms, let alone communicate their own sexual needs and desires. Small wonder, when our early learning about sex has generally come from parental and religious prohibitions, and from pornography and peer groups. All of these "teachings" are based on fantasy, exaggeration and misinformation. Men are wrongly led to believe that they should know how to be great lovers without any instruction or feedback. Many men are embarrassed to admit that they are floundering sexually and don't know exactly what their partner wants. They are unable to ask their partners what would please them due to false perceptions about masculinity, and even see it as insulting and upsetting when their partner asks for something specific or tells them what to do. And for women, even now in the twenty-first century, a double standard still exists. If they try to express their sexual desires and openly enjoy their sexuality, they frequently are seen as demanding, overly aggressive, cheap and unladylike.

Isn't it interesting that when our back itches, not only can we ask our partner to scratch it, but we are also very clear in communicating exactly which spot to scratch and how to do it ("higher, to the left, harder") and how long to keep doing it ("don't stop yet; more")? Yet when it comes to communicating our sexual needs, many of us become mute because we fear that communicating those things puts our manhood ,womanhood or even our realtionship on the line. However, if we don't honestly communicate what feels good to us and what arouses us, the odds of getting what we want are low.

The irony is that often we believe we are communicating our sexual needs, wants and desires in a clear way – and yet the messages are either unheard or misunderstood or often clouded by differences in sexual terminology. We are left with frustration, anger and pain, wondering why our partner will not give us what we want. If they really loved us, we think, they would instinctively know our unspoken desires! Often we pull away and put up emotional walls. Meanwhile, our partner may be left wishing they were psychic. If only they could just figure out what it is that we want, then everything would be okay. To be a good communicator, you can't rely on reading minds. Instead, you need to use some of the essential communication techniques we recommend below.

C P R:

C

P

R

Before you begin any communication exercise, be sure to set an environment conducive for it. This includes turning off all electronics that may distract you, such as the TV, radio and cell phones. Also be sure that the kids and pets are taken care of so they won't interrupt you. Then sit comfortably facing each other and begin communicating using the model below.

Effective communication relies upon three basic elements:

1) sending a message

2) receiving a message

3) understanding a message.

SENDING A MESSAGE:

- *Politely get your partner's attention.*

- *Use "I" messages in expressing self. (For example, "I feel unimportant and hurt when I'm not listened to" rather than "You selfish, insensitive pig! You never pay attention to me when I speak to you!")*

- *Clearly and concisely state the facts of the issue at hand.*

- *State how the issue has affected you.*

- *Take ownership by expressing your feelings about the facts.*

- *Ask for what you want.*

- *Acknowledge success for your efforts.*

- *Let your partner know when you're done.*

RECEIVING A MESSAGE:

- *Take care of yourself so you do not get lost in your feelings.*

- *Focus on being there for your partner rather then memorizing or preparing to respond.*

- *Make eye contact.*

- *Occasionally nod and say, "um-hum." This does not mean you agree; instead it shows you're listening and paying attention.*

- *Paraphrase back what you heard.*

- *Ask for clarification when needed.*

- *Empathize with your partner's feelings.*

UNDERSTANDING A MESSAGE:

Be sure your partner knows what you're talking about, especially if you use slang terms for sexual activities or body parts.

Communicate your desires with detail. For example, don't say: "I want you to show me that you love me." It's too vague. Instead say "You can show me that you love me by rubbing my back every night." Ask your partner to repeat to you what they think you just said or asked for and correct any misinterpretations or omissions.

If you and your partner are unaccustomed to communicating about your innermost feelings and desires, test the waters slowly and carefully until these techniques become more familiar. Practice communicating about less threatening topics, such as where to vacation or who to invite for Thanksgiving dinner. Slowly work up to more highly charged issues. It is helpful to set up appointments to communicate on the more sensitive issues so that you get your partner's full, uninterrupted attention. Be aware, however, that the fact that you communicate your needs to your partner does not obligate your partner to fulfill them.

You are working with this CPR program because you both want a more loving and happy life together. So approach each communication with self-care and caring for your partner. Create a safety net or a comfort zone for each other. Share your thoughts and feelings without shame, blame, guilt or harsh words and validate each other and empathize with each other's feelings.

Make a list of at least three things that you would like to communicate to your partner:

C

P

R

1. _____

2. _____

3. _____

COMMITMENT

Many relationships fall apart because one or both partners do not exhibit commitment to each other or the relationship. Instead, they exhibit apathy or a sense that they have one foot out the door if their partner doesn't "shape up." To make this process work, you must both make a commitment to see it through. You must let your partner know that you are in the relationship for the long haul. This means that you will be persistent in working to improve your sex life, even if things get tough or painful. This commitment builds trust in your partner and the relationship. Try seeing difficulties that may arise as speed bumps rather than brick walls. By slowing down and preparing, you can navigate over the bumps and keep going.

Contracts help solidify a couple's commitment by giving each partner a written document to view and fall back on. Having our partner's signature on an agreement adds legitimacy and shows their willingness to work on the relationship. The knowledge that our partner has agreed to be fully involved with us in attempting to revitalize our relationship provides us with a sense of safety and assurance which, in turn, permits us to do the work and make the changes that the CPR program will require.

C P R:

A tool that many couples find useful in demonstrating their committment to each other is a contract. Basically, the contract includes agreement by both partners to do certain things to strengthen their relationship.(For example "We agree to do the CPR assignments at least 3 times a week, even if we're not in the mood" or "We agree to check in with each other on our progress, at least once a week.") The contract should also include a consequence for not following through with the contract (eg. "We will seek professional help to work through our impasse") and a reward for following through (eg. "We will go out for dinner without the kids."). The contract should be signed and dated, and reviewed and revised periodically.

To get started, sit down with your partner and discuss the elements that you each feel are important to include. Then fill them in on the contract below.

COMMITMENT CONTRACT

1. We agree to _____

2. We agree to _____

3. We agree to _____

4. We agree to _____

Consequence(s) for following through/not following through with this contract:

_____

_____

Start Date: _____ *Review Date:* _____

Signature: _____ *Date:* _____

Signature: _____ *Date:* _____

CHANGE

It's time for change to take place in your relationship. What you've been doing until now has not been working. If it were, you would not be reading this CPR book. You would not have to read it because your sex life would be vibrant and passion-filled.

Americans are used to quick fixes, fast food and thirty-second sound bytes. Unfortunately, relationships don't work that way. It takes time to change long-standing behavior patterns.

We know that change is difficult and scary. As much as people want to change, there is often the fear of facing the unknown. Most people find that staying with the unhappy status quo is more comfortable than taking risks and stabs at the new and, often anxiety-provoking, unknown. However, if you work together on implementing change, you are bound to maximize your chances for success.

C P R:

Try thinking about (and, if necessary, altering) your attitudes toward change. Focus on the positive aspect of how new behaviors and insights will improve your relationship, instead of fearing how the changes could backfire.

Also, accept the reality of who your partner is. Recognize that some of your partner's behaviors may never change and that you may have to be the one to compromise. Instead of hoping that your partner will change, identify ways in which you are willing to change. Most of the changes you will be incorporating will come from your checklists, as this is what you and your partner have already identified as keys to success.

Take one item from that list that seems to be the easiest or the least risky. Start with that one. Give yourself a big pat on the back after you've accomplished it!

Go back and look at the items on your partner's checklist right now.

Write the one you will work on today on this line:

_____

Next, write three specific things you will do to make this item from your partner's checklist happen. For example, if you picked "call me pet names," you might now choose to write:

• *I will ask her what pet names she likes.*

• *I will write her favorite pet names and carry a list of them in my wallet.*

• *I will keep the list of her favorite pet names next to my computer.*

• *I will use these pet names daily when talking to her.*

What I will do to make the item from my partner's checklist happen:

_____

_____

COITUS (INTERCOURSE)

Coitus, more commonly known as penis-in-vagina intercourse, is what people generally think of when they think of the word sex; it's what many see as the "real thing." After all, intercourse is a wonderful activity that feels physically good and leaves most people feeling more intimately connected with their partners.

You may very well have been thinking that intercourse, or more frequent intercourse, was the main goal when you purchased this book. For most of you, this will probably be the case. However, if you rush to have intercourse while working on the early stages of this book, you may very well find yourself right back where you started – disinterested, dissatisfied and resentful.

In most relationships where sex is dead, dying or dull, one partner is typically much less interested (if at all) in sexual contact. This partner may be feeling extreme pressure from the other to engage in intercourse and, as a result, may feel even less interested. The more sexually interested partner will typically be struggling with frustration, anger and disappointment. While this partner may sometimes turn away from sex altogether or pursue sex elsewhere, they will more likely increase efforts to pursue the less interested one in a desperate attempt to keep sex alive, causing tension in the relationship.

C P R:

As a couple, agree to put a ban on intercourse until you have reached the final chapter of this book, where this sexual activity is reintroduced. This suggestion may evoke groans from some of you, but we assure you that it is a tried-and-true sex therapy method that works for most couples. Adhering to the ban removes what is a source of conflict and pain in your relationship. By slowly doing the CPR suggestions in this book and integrating the ones that are significant to you into your life, you will enrich your relationship. By the time you reintroduce coitus, it will be a much more meaningful and enjoyable experience, because you will have learned your partner's needs and conditions for good sex and how to fulfill them.

Discuss this temporary ban on intercourse with your partner. See if you can both view it as an investment in a long-lasting, healthy sex life rather than some sort of deprivation. A short contract agreeing to this ban may be written and look something like this:

We, Jill and Jack, agree to refrain from coitus with each other until we reach the CPR recommending that we reintroduce it back into our sex life.

Jill's signature: _____ Date: _____

Jack's signature: _____ Date: _____

Now write your own "ban on coitus" contract here and sign it.

_____

_____

Signature: _____ Date: _____

Signature: _____ Date: _____

Now that you have uncovered some of your own recipes for resuscitating your sex life, what follows, for the remainder of the book, are our suggestions. These are things that have historically worked successfully for our sex therapy clients. We expect these suggestion will work equally well for you.

NOTES:

_____

_____

_____

_____

_____

_____

_____

_____

_____

CHAPTER 2

C
P
R

The C's

CARESS

CELEBRATE CHARTING

CHILDREN CLEANLINESS COMPANY'S COMING

COMPENSATE COMPLIMENT COMPROMISE CONDIMENTS

CONDITIONS FOR GOOD SEX CONTENTMENT COUNT YOUR BLESSINGS

CARESS

A lack of touch, or infrequent touch, may have contributed significantly to the deterioration of your sex life. Most of us want to touch, and be touched by, the people we love. During courtship, we thrill to our partner's caresses, equating them to a demonstration of love. Sadly, for many couples, touch dwindles after the early days of a relationship.

We often feel unloved when we are not touched, or are touched only during sex In the latter case, caressing appears to be merely a means to initiate sex, rather than an expression of nurturing and caring. This can create an emotional and physical distancing from our partner, making us resistant to sex. Furthermore, when we are caressed only during sex, we assume that caressing inevitably leads to intercourse. So it follows that, no matter how much we would like to touch, if we want to avoid intercourse, we will refrain from caressing our partner.

Strong bonds are formed through touch. Our skin is our body's largest sensory organ, and it requires at least as much stimulation as any other sense organ. Extensive research by anthropologist Ashley Montagu shows that an infant needs to be held and touched in order to develop emotionally and physically. Serious consequences can occur when children are not held and lovingly touched early in life. Organ systems and muscles may begin to atrophy, deformity may occur and developmental and physical growth may be delayed. For adults, while atrophy of the organs or spine will not occur from lack of touch, what can happen instead is a more spiritual type of atrophy, such as deep sadness, longing, and feelings of being undesirable and unlovable.

In a relationship, caressing speaks volumes. It shows your partner that you care, that you are concerned about their well-being. It connects partners – no matter their age – in a deeply-felt way, both physically and emotionally. Remember, you are never too old to touch or to want to be touched. It is a lifelong need.

C P R:

    While keeping your clothes on, take turns being the giver and the receiver of touch. As the giver, for at least ten minutes, gently stroke your partner's face, head, or neck. Next do the same with the arms, hands, legs or feet – or several of these body parts in the same session.

    After you have tried this CPR exercise a few times, use massage oil or cream to change the sensation for you and your partner. As you receive touch, give your partner feedback. Let them know what kind of touching pleases you. You can also demonstrate this to your partner by touching them the way you yourself would like to be touched.

    Don't limit your caressing to the bedroom. Make a commitment to reach out and touch your partner during routine activities, such as when you are watching TV, in the car or in a restaurant; and hold hands when you are out for a stroll together or at the movies.

C

P

R

CELEBRATE

Sexual and relationship growth is often hard work. It can become a miserable chore if all you do is keep working on it! This is especially true if you continue to focus on the failures, the disappointments, the and "if onlys."

It's important to celebrate your successes as you proceed through this book. Don't wait until you've finished reading it. You've already accomplished things worth celebrating. You've taken steps toward regaining a happy sex life. You've completed the checkup and the checklist, are communicating to each other in a new way and you are caressing each other as well. That's worth a big pat on the back!

Celebrating can bring joy to your relationship. Even if you don't find the success that you were hoping for in a romantic or sexual encounter, celebrate the fact that you tried. You can always celebrate again when the encounter or CPR assignment does turn out the way you want it to! Make the celebration of your success a routine part of working with this CPR book.

C P R:

Celebrate yourselves! You have earned it. Give each other a high five, a toast or a passionate kiss. Discuss together the ways in which you celebrate other things in your lives. For example, do you go out for a special meal, throw a party, buy or make a plaque? In the space below, write three ways the two of you will celebrate:

C

P

R

1. _____

2. _____

3. _____

CHARTING

In 1492 Christopher Columbus set sail from Spain to chart a new route to India. We know that he didn't make it. Nevertheless, like all great adventurers, he took his time, carefully explored everything he encountered, and charted the location of mountains, lakes, oceans and other landmarks. The new discoveries were no doubt exciting for him.

Exploring and charting your partner's body for the first time was probably very exciting. With time, however, we stop exploring the familiar landscape of our partner's body, believing we've seen all there is to see and that there's nothing new to discover. But landscapes change over time – and so do we. Going back and charting afresh will most certainly bear new fruit.

C P R:

C
P
R

Chart your partner again, or for the first time. Decide who will go first. Who will be the explorer, and who will be explored? If you are the explorer, have your partner lie down comfortably. Explain to them that the only intent of this exercise is to chart the "territory". It is not something that will lead to sex. Stating this from the beginning can ease any perceived pressure that it will lead to something your partner may not want to do; it will also alleviate any pressure to perform. Tell your partner to relax and to let you know if anything feels uncomfortable. As the explorer, you choose where to begin and where to end; but be sure that you leave no part of your partner's body uncharted (except for the genitals, which will be charted in the Advanced CPR chapter).

Imagine that you have never seen or touched your partner before. Look at the "terrain" and gently touch what you see. You may want to use two fingers or your entire hand. Feel the differences in texture, warmth and responsiveness of the various body parts. You may want to smell and taste the parts you discover.

Verbally share what you find with your partner as you are exploring. Let them know what their body looks like, what if feels like and what it tastes like. Now switch roles and give your partner a chance to chart you. Another time, do your charting with oils, creams, feathers, furs or anything that will maximize the experience for you and your partner.

If receiving or giving was difficult for you, hang in no mater how much you'd like to abandon this CPR. Communicate with your partner what it would take to make this experience more comfortable for you. Learning the intricacies of our partner's body is an opportunity that many couples not reading this book would love to have. They just don't know how to suggest it or go about it. So take full advantage of this assignment and become an expert on the "terrain" and how to tend to it.

CHEERLEADING

Clients frequently complain that their partner never offers words of support, or that they only give suggestions for improvement when trying to be supportive. Throughout this CPR process we need to know that our partners are our cheerleaders and are supporting us in our efforts to make our relationship and our sex lives better.

Cheerleading is a necessary tool. It is how we build self-esteem in our children and how we keep it alive in our partners. It motivates us to do our best. It builds a sense of team effort and reminds us that we are not alone – that our partner believes in us and wants to see us succeed. We tend to feel closer to our cheerleader and are more willing to be intimate with those who are proud of us and provide us with emotional support.

C P R:

Think about the ways in which you would like to hear your partner cheer you on.

For example, Jill wrote for Jack:

- *I'm very proud of your accomplishments at work.*

- *Great job on making such a splendid meal, sweetheart!*

- *I really like how you massage me. You have great hands!*

Now write three of your own:

1. _____

2. _____

3. _____

Discuss these with your partner and then use them when the opportunity arises.

Now that you have identified acceptable cheers, seize opportunities every day to give verbal encouragement and support to your partner. Be your partner's number one fan and cheerleader!

Also, start each CPR exercise with an encouraging couple cheer. For example, you may want to look at each other and shout: "All right, here we go! We can do it! Regardless of the outcome, we will be successful for trying. Yeah, team!"

CHERISH

Unfortunately, once we are in a marriage or a committed relationship, many of us start to take our partners for granted. The courtship is over – and now there is no need to try any more. We stop cherishing our partner, and the intimacy and passion in the relationship begin to fade and die. When we cherish our partner, we see and treat them as if they were a work of art, a precious jewel or something else that we value. Cherishing behaviors show your partner that they are special and that you treasure them. In most cases, this increases receptivity to sexual advances.

C P R:

C
P
R

Think of something in life that takes your breath away, that inspires you with awe when you see it. Greet your partner any time you've been apart and are now coming back together as if they were that special thing. Gaze at them with awe. Touch and treat your partner tenderly as if they were a delicate treasure. Let your partner know that you love and admire them and that they are cherished.

Do this CPR even if you feel silly or uncomfortable treating your partner in this manner. The benefits to both of you can be enormous.

CHILDREN

While children bring us great joy, they can also negatively impact our sex lives. New parents find little time for sex. Couples are faced with the daunting tasks of caring for a newborn on little or no sleep, with extra chores to do, with the challenges of feeding (bottle or breast) and often a new person in the bed. In addition, most women need to recover from the pain of childbirth before sex can be enjoyed.

As children age, new sexual challenges present themselves. The couple may refrain from sex out of fear that the child will hear them having sex, or walk in without knocking and catch them in the heat of passion. Jealousy may crop up for one of the partners if the child becomes either "daddy's little girl" or "mommy's little boy." The teenage years and dating, cars and drugs engender issues that frequently result in fights and can often dampen sexual energy between the parents.

When children grow up and leave the home, some parents are left with the "empty nest syndrome." While this sometimes brings sexual partners together, as they now are free to openly enjoy sex again, many find the loneliness too much and find themselves drifting even further apart sexually.

C P R:

C

P

R

Be sure to make your couple time (including time for romance and sex) a priority. Having private time together, dates alone, weekend getaways and vacations is essential. Find a babysitter or a family member or friend to take care of the kids. Keep in mind that you are not abandoning your children. They will still be there when you return and you will be more refreshed and more ready to give them your attention.

Teach your children to respect closed doors. Parents and children alike need and deserve private time. Model loving behaviors for your children by nurturing your relationship with each other. Remember that your children will still love you if you spend time loving each other. In fact, when they are grown, they may remember your closeness as one of the best things from their childhood!

CLEANLINESS

While certain clients report that natural body odors, such as sweat, are a turn-on for them, most report that poor personal hygiene is a turn-off. Bad breath, strong body odor and pungent genital odors keep many people from enjoying pleasurable sexual activities. Women typically love it when a man is clean-shaven and has clean fingernails. Men are strongly attracted to women who smell pretty, whose hair is clean and shiny and whose breath is sweet. It is commonly said that "cleanliness is next to godliness," and it is true that cleanliness certainly is vital if you want to be viewed as a sex god or goddess by your partner.

C P R:

Make an effort to look your very best for your partner at all times. If you have to greet your partner while you are not at your best, tell them you would like to get ready for them and see if they can wait while you take a shower, brush your teeth, change your clothes or freshen up.

Alternatively, cleansing your partner can be great fun, and very sensuous as well! It can alleviate your concerns about their hygiene and about performing oral sex. Take a bath or shower together and wash each other all over, and all over again! Leave no part untouched. Afterward, dry each other and rub lotions or sprinkle powder onto each other.

COMPANY'S COMING

As a rule, when we are expecting company, we clean the house, use special plates and glasses, and cook more elaborate meals. We do the same thing when we invite a date over for dinner. We make special efforts. We want to impress our our date, make them feel at home, and ensure that they enjoy themselves. These preparations also build excitement and anticipation for our company's or date's arrival.

However, few of us continue to do these things past the early stages of a new relationship. Thus, coming home no longer feels special, nor is it something to look forward to; and seeing your partner walk in the door isn't nearly as exciting as it used to be.

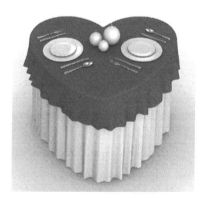

C P R:

Pick a day when you can take the time to go the extra distance. On that day, dress nicely and make, or buy, a meal and dessert that your partner really likes. Prepare the house by playing special music, arranging flowers and cleaning away clutter. Clear your schedule and be prepared to let the answering machine pick up messages. If you are grumpy, put on a happy face and greet your partner in the same manner that you would treat a welcome guest. Turn off the TV, leave the computer alone and devote your full attention to your partner. Treat them like special company.

List three ways that you are going to treat your partner like company:

1. _____

2. _____

3. _____

Compensate
FOR LACK OF EDUCATION

Sex therapy is frequently considered to be 80% education. Why so much? Despite living in a modern society in which sex is discussed so often, most Americans lack some very fundamental information regarding sexuality. For example, parents are reluctant to discuss actual facts about sex with their children. And "abstinence only" sex education in schools is not sex education at all. It offers few facts, much incorrect information, and fails to cover the basics for maintaining a healthy and intimate sexual relationship. Most Americans learn about sex from stories their peers share, from the media and from pornography – all of which lack a basis in reality. As a result, most of us do not have correct information about sex and feel insecure and inadequate in the bedroom.

C P R:

Discuss and decide upon what, if any, areas of sexuality you would like to be better informed about. Next, go to web sites such as www.siecus.org, the web site for the Sex Information and Education Counsel of the United States (SIECUS), or www.aasect.org, the web site for the American Association of Sexuality Educators, Counselors and Therapists (AASECT). A prime purpose of both of these organizations is to provide access to the most accurate and up-to-date information on sexuality. You will find links to download free files on a wide variety of topics within the field of sexuality as well as links to sites where you can purchase books that these organizations endorse. After you've completed some reading, write down three things you've learned that help you feel more sexually informed and secure.

Jot down three areas that you would like to be better informed about. Discuss your findings with your partner.

1. _____

2. _____

3. _____

Write down any new things that you learned from investigating these areas.

_____

_____

_____

COMPLIMENT

Over time, couples settle into a sense of security and stop complimenting each other. When we are in a close relationship with someone who seldom, or never, gives us compliments, we tend to feel unappreciated. This is all the more true if all we hear is criticism and disapproval. Our efforts in the relationship seem to be made in vain and go unnoticed. Apathy can easily follow. This is especially true if we witness our partner's frequent compliments to others.

Compliments make us feel good by giving us validation for who we are and what we do. Everyone likes to feel appreciated. When compliments from our partner are in ample supply, our self-esteem rises and we are much more motivated to give love and appreciation in exchange. Compliments are like aphrodisiacs. They are important before, during and after sex:

•Before sex: "Ah, you smell wonderful. I can't wait to be close to you."

•During sex: "Oh, that feels so good. Your touch is wonderful."

•After sex: "Honey, you are the best lover. That was great!"

C P R:

Decide what you think is your partner's best physical features (for example, really strong hands, twinkling eyes, soft skin, good smell, beautiful hair). Write three of them here:

1. _____

2. _____

3. _____

Next think of something your partner recently did for you that you really appreciate (for example, they cooked a fantastic meal, helped you with your chores, and brought you your coffee each morning). Write three of them here:

1. _____

2. _____

3. _____

Now give these compliments to your partner liberally. It's important for our partners to hear that we are proud of them and value them. **Remember that your partner can't know what qualities you value in them unless you tell them.** *If your partner is giving you compliments, be sure to accept them graciously. A simple "thank you," or "I really appreciate you saying that," will go a long way. Consider offering at least one compliment per day to your partner!*

COMPROMISE

Healthy relationships must include compromise. It's unrealistic to expect or hope that a relationship will always be based upon your decisions, needs and wants. Both partners need to be considered. Although this means sometimes giving up control and not always getting everything you want, it's certainly not a losing proposition. The relationship gains when the partners find a way to neutralize issues that were a source of stress.

Compromise comes in two basic forms. There is a compromise in which both partners give up some things to find the middle ground. "I want a big dog, you want a small dog. We'll get a medium-sized dog and love it just the same." Or you can do a joint effort where each of you takes turns making compromises. "I'll go to the baseball game with you tonight if you go to the concert with me tomorrow."

C P R:

While you cannot always compromise when it comes to sex, you may be surprised by how often you can. First, try this CPR with something non-sexual, such as who to invite to a dinner party, the color to paint a room in the house, or where to go on a vacation. Write down three things you are willing to compromise on:

1. _____

2. _____

3. _____

Now, building on your success, make a similar list of three relationship issues you are willing to compromise on, such as when or how often to do the CPR assignments or what sensual or romantic activities you are willing to engage in. Write them here:

1. _____

2. _____

3. _____

Now pick one item from each of your lists and see if you can "cut a deal" and compromise as you did before. Were you successful? If so, try this same process with more sexually explicit issues when you're instructed to work on them later in this CPR book. If not, go back to making compromises on non-relationship issues for a while, until you build up confidence negotiating them.

CONDIMENTS

Condiments are used to flavor and spice food. Condiments like salt, pepper, salsa, horseradish and other sauces complement a meal and give it extra taste. Meals without any condiments are bland and lack originality and taste. The same can be true when it comes to your sex life. If your sex life is dull or dying, things such as sweet words, music, clothing, books, visual aids or sex toys act as condiments which can spice up and enhance a typical sexual encounter. In fact, every CPR suggestion in this book is in itself a condiment! For example, caressing is a perfect condiment to a healthy sexual encounter.

C P R:

The purpose of this exercise is to add several condiments to your sensual and sexual repertoire. For any CPR exercise in this book, try to enhance it by introducing condiments of your own choosing or borrowing some from the recommended "C" list below.

C

P

R

- *Chocolates or candies*

- *Champagne or wine*

- *Cologne or perfume*

- *Chocolate syrup, honey or whipped cream*

- *CDs, clips or cassettes of your favorite music*

- *Creams, lotions and massage oils*

- *Carnations, calla lilies or other flowers*

- *Clothing that entices*

- *Cards, notes and letters*

- *Calls to say, "I love you"*

CONDITIONS FOR GOOD SEX

Everyone has conditions that add to – or distract from – making sex fulfilling. Some of these conditions are so common that they are assumed to be universal, and it is thought that everyone requires or desires them. For example, to really enjoy sex, most women require a positive, committed relationship filled with respect, good treatment outside the bedroom, and romance. Men want sex at any time and in any place. They want an enthusiastic partner who really enjoys sex, compliments their sexual abilities, and – of course – expects the activity to end with his orgasm. While these generalizations may be true for some of us, it is not fair to assume that they apply to everyone.

There are many other conditions a person may feel are important for their enjoyment of sex. Lots of these other conditions may have nothing to do with the sexual acts themselves, but more to do with timing, responsibility or health. For example, many of us need total privacy, the kids safely tucked in for the night, the room temperature just right, or special pillows to support our aching backs.

When our conditions are seldom, if ever, met, desire for sex diminishes; and when sex does occur, it is not nearly as satisfying as it could be. So, if you would like to have quality sex that is tailored to your needs, it's important to recognize your conditions and communicate them to your partner. If each of you can have as many as possible of your conditions satisfied, lovemaking will become something that you look forward to, rather than something that you try to avoid.

C P R:

What do you absolutely need in order to relax and be able to get excited enough to enjoy sex? This may be a bit difficult for men to answer because according to the misinformation put forth by the media, they are not supposed to have conditions at all – just a willing partner. How far from the truth this is!

Some of your conditions may already be on your checklist, but others may not. Update your checklist to make it contain conditions for good sex. Don't feel that any of your conditions are stupid or shameful, or that you already have too many. If these things are important to you, they should be on the list. But don't include items that are unrealistic or potentially offensive

Now write three conditions for good sex in order of priority here.

1. _____

2. _____

3. _____

Next share the lists with each other, much like you did in the beginning of this book. See if you can agree to a few things from both lists and incorporate them into your next lovemaking session. And, don't forget to thank your partner for their attempts to fulfill your conditions for good sex.

CONTENTMENT

Those of us who are content with what we have are fortunate. Sadly, many of us see the glass as half empty and think the grass is always greener on the other side. Our discontentment extends to our homes, our jobs, our possessions, our children, our spouses and of course, our sex lives. We exhaust ourselves trying to compete with neighbors, friends or colleagues. Where sex is concerned, we fantasize that we would be happier if our partner were a celebrity like Brad Pitt or Angelina Jolie, or someone younger, more muscular, sexier or thinner.

Sure. There are probably better-looking, sexier people in the world than your partner, but do you really think that if you were to spend the rest of your life with them, you would be any happier than you are now with your partner? Would you not also have in-law issues and bills and taxes to pay? Consider how superficial and media-dependent our perception of beauty is, and then think of all the ways in which your partner's beauty goes deeper than any one of them.

C P R:

Think of the last time you were at an art museum, an art gallery or art show. Remember something you saw that you admired tremendously and thought was strikingly beautiful. As you relished in the sight of this fine piece you probably also considered what it would be like to take it home with you. You most likely weighed the cost of the item, considered how it would or would not fit into your own home, thought of the wonderful things you already have, and, finally decided that you can appreciate the art without having to have it. When you got home you might have then looked at the items you already have and appreciated them for what they are. You valued your current art as it already fit in your home and you may also have remembered the joy you had when you obtained it.

Now do the same thing with people other than your partner you find yourself attracted to. Think of how they might really fit into your life, what it would cost you if you pursued them and how there are millions of people out there that you imagine you would love to be with, at least in a sexual way. Write down cost things you would have to sacrifice in your life if you pursued another lover in life regardless of giving up, or not giving up, the partner you currently have.

1. _____

2. _____

3. _____

Next, look closely at your own partner. Consider the wonderful things you get from being with them. Remember what it was like finding them in the first place, what attracted you to them and how well they fit into your life now. Write some of these thoughts below and then be sure to tell your partner why you are so content to have them in your life.

1. _____

2. _____

3. _____

COUNT YOUR BLESSINGS

Focusing only on the negative parts of life in life is self-defeating. It leads to bitterness, anger and depression. You may have spent countless hours thinking negatively about your partner. You may have been blaming them for the lack of sex and closeness, and pulled away from them emotionally and physically. Clearly there is room to refocus, to look at the good things your partner does and the efforts they are making to work with you on solving the relationship problems; in other words, count your blessings. By doing so, you are more likely to feel good about yourself, your partner and your relationship.

C P R:

Think about the things you love about your partner and why you want to continue your relationship with them. List these blessings below.

1. _____

2. _____

3. _____

4. _____

5. _____

Keep this list in your purse or wallet and carry it with you throughout the day. Pull out your list and review it whenever you find yourself feeling discouraged about the lack of intimacy. Begin and end each day by reviewing your list to reinforce your knowledge of your blessings.

COURTSHIP

Apathy tends to creep into relationships over time. Partners begin to take each other for granted. How often do you ask your partner out on a date? After all, you've already been living together for years. And how often do you write your partner love letters or send a sexy text message or e-mail or give them little "just because" gifts?

However small they are, courtship behaviors have tremendous power in enhancing a relationship. They focus attention on pleasing our partner and add substantially to a sense of being wanted and cared for to the one receiving them. Sound familiar? You may have listed some of these courtship behaviors on your checklist. Courtship is a form of foreplay and is a major element is resuscitating a sexual relationship.

C P R:

Pretend you are single and call up your partner and ask them out on a date. Be flirtatious and romantic in your speech as you make these arrangements. Phone, e-mail or text-message your partner a couple days in advance to confirm your date. Show up for the date as if it was your first with your partner. Bring a little something special If necessary, leave the house and come back to pick up your date.

During the date hold hands, gaze into each other's eyes. Focus your full attention on your date and show an interest in them, and what they have to say. Do this every week for a month, taking turns with being the inviter and the invitee. When you are the inviter, take charge and make all the decisions as to where to go and what to do on the date, but try to choose activities that would please your partner as well.

Remember you don't have to make the dates elaborate and expensive, especially as you develop this weekly habit into an ongoing practice that will endure throughout the life of your relationship.

Plan two dates and write down the details below.

CUDDLE

Like caressing, cuddling or hugging helps us feel nourished, cared for, loved and protected. Similarly, a lack of cuddling or only cuddling during sexual activities leaves us feeling disconnected. We sometimes avoid this activity altogether as we falsely believe that if we engage in cuddling then we must take the next step and have intercourse.

As opposed to caressing, cuddling is a more intimate activity. It is not just touching with your fingers but rather involves full body contact. On the simplest level it helps us literally feel warm with our partners. Cuddling is an important and relatively safe part of a couple's life together, even when sex is absent. Cuddling also helps sexually active couples feel emotionally closer and creates a sense of oneness.

C P R:

Start by cuddling on the couch. If you are not on the couch at this moment, go there, right now. Turn on the TV or some music and cuddle. Hold each other close, put an arm around your partner's shoulder or lie down with your head on your partner's chest or lap. Don't reach for the genitals. Simply hold your partner and caress them lightly. This is a safe, non-threatening way of being close for most.

As you reintroduce sexual activity into your relationship, start and finish each encounter by spooning – a form of cuddling in which both partners lie on their same sides facing the same direction, one in front of the other, with the knees curled partially upward toward the chest. The person in back wraps the upper arm around the person in front, and the person in front holds their partner's hand over their heart or chest. Add synchronized breathing, matching your partner's inhalation and exhalation pattern, so that the two of you feel as if you are one. For now, you can achieve similar physical closeness by doing this CPR clothed.

C

P

R

NOTES:

_____

_____

_____

_____

_____

_____

_____

_____

_____

_____

CHAPTER 3

C
P
R

The P's

PACKAGING

PALS   PAMPER

PARTICIPATION   PASSION

PATIENCE   PEACEFULNESS   PEEL

PERFORMANCE ANXIETY   PERMISSION

PERSEVERANCE   PETS   PETTING   PHOBIAS

PILLOW TALK   PLAN   PLAY   PLEASE   PRACTICE

PREFERENCE   PRETENDING   PRIME TIME   PRIORITIZE   PROFESSIONALS

PROHIBITION   PROLONG   PROSE AND POETRY   PUCKER UP   PURR

PACKAGING

Familiarity often breeds laziness when it comes to our dress style. We tend to let ourselves go. Why should we wear something nice when we are having dinner at home with our partner of many years? There's a good reason: packaging says a lot! Food is more appetizing when given the right presentation. Gifts are more enticing when dressed up with fancy wrappings; clothing works the same way.

Remember when you were first dating, how much time you spent grooming yourself before the date? You certainly would not have greeted your date at the door in sweats and with your hair a mess! You probably would have thought twice before going to their house straight from the gym without first showering and putting on clean clothes. You made an effort to look your best. You wanted to make a good impression, so you packaged yourself in an appealing and enticing way. Do the same thing to re-entice your partner!

C P R:

Greet your partner after being apart for the day, a few days or a week or more, with clothing that says "I'm excited to see you." You don't have to spend a lot of money on new clothing or wear something that is too sexy or uncomfortable. Discuss with each other what clothes you already have that your partner favors on you. Pick items from those favorites that are appropriate for the activities of your day and wear them for your partner. And, to enhance the package, don't forget to pay attention to your personal hygiene.

At times, surprise your partner by wearing something new and overtly sexy. If you pick lingerie or underwear, let your partner undress you and see your purchase for the first time.

Write down three items of clothing you already have that will convey enticement to your partner. If you don't have anything enticing in your wardrobe, go out and buy three things and write them here.

C
P
R

1. _____

2. _____

3. _____

PALS

It's amazing how many couples spend years and years living under the same roof, and yet are not friends. They have lost the friendship that they most likely had during their early days together and have become more like roommates. They each have their own jobs, workout schedules and outside interests. When they get together at night, they discuss the kids or pets and then watch TV, read or sit at the computer. They appear together at family functions and social occasions, but a certain important connection is missing.

Many people find it difficult to have good sex or remain lovers with somebody who is not their friend. Romance may have attracted you to your partner, but friendship is the glue that can solidify the relationship and make it last. The ultimate compliment we can give to our partner is "you are my best friend and lover."

C P R:

Ask questions, listen, and empathize with your partner and show an interest in them. Share your feelings with each other. Accept your partner for who they are and give support and encouragement to them for their dreams and endeavors. Comfort them when they are sad or scared. That's what pals do.

Ask them how their day was. Ask them if they need anything or want to discuss anything that has been weighing on them. Ask them to take a class with you, share a hobby, or participate in an activity. Go for a walk, see a movie, read a book together, play cards or just sit around and catch up.

Write down three things you would want from someone who is a pal:

1. _____

2. _____

3. _____

Share this with your partner, ask if they will do these things for you, and try hard to do the three things your partner asks you to do, as a friend, as a pal. Remember- friendship involves a lot of mutual give and take.

PAMPER

People involved in long-term relationships who wind up having affairs with someone else quite often report that they took advantage of the opportunity because they felt neglected and taken for granted by their partner. We frequently hear such things as, "Sure, he's a great guy, a wonderful father, a hard worker, but he never makes me feel special!" Or they may say, "She's sexy and a great cook. But what good is it if she pays no attention to me?"

It's hard to stay interested in someone when there is a sense that they are neglecting us. So how do you show your special someone that you're still interested in them if you are already cooking for them, helping around the house and perhaps having occasional sex with them? Pampering can help.

Everyone deserves a little spoiling now and then. When we pamper our partners, we cater to and indulge them. A partner's pampering can make us feel so nurtured and loved that it puts us in the mood for sexual intimacy.

C P R:

Pamper your partner. Give them a sensuous massage, footbath or sponge bath. Make a special dinner, pour wine, light candles and have their favorite music playing in the background. Buy them little gifts. Do some of their usual chores or pay someone to do those chores. Watch your partner's response and make sure they are comfortable and pleased. Discuss afterward if there is anything more they need in order to feel fully pampered.

Make a pledge to yourself to pamper your partner daily.

List three things that you will do in order to pamper your partner.

1. _____

2. _____

3. _____

List three things that you would like your partner to do to pamper you.

1. _____

2. _____

3. _____

PARTICIPATION

Many people in relationships are like two ships passing in the night. Each partner has so many solo activities that they do in the course of the week that they barely see each other. The relationship seems to be low on their priority scale. This over-involvement in things other than the relationship itself often creates emotional and sexual distance between the partners. One or both partners may think that the other is failing to participate in the relationship and they feel hurt, frustrated, let down and not at all interested in being sexually intimate.

C P R:

There are activities that involve our bodies and our sexuality that we typically see as solo activities – washing ourselves, dressing and undressing, or masturbating. Likewise, many of us have hobbies and activities outside the home that we do on our own. Joining our partner in some of these activities may be playful and educational and will certainly create more quality time together.

Join your partner in their favorite activity or hobby, even if it means taking classes to learn it. Think of all the extra time you will have together and how much your partner will appreciate your participation.

At bath time, offer to shampoo, dry and brush your partner's hair.

You can also have fun by choosing your partner's undergarments or outfit and dress them or else undress them at the end of the day.

You can participate in your partner's masturbation by holding their hand, kissing them, stroking them or handing them items they might want to use. It may take some time to get over the initial discomfort, but once you do, the experience can be educational for you and arousing for both of you.

Write three things that you would like to start doing with your partner.

1. _____

2. _____

3. _____

PASSION

We so often hear our clients complain that their partner goes through all the right motions and yet, something is lacking – there is no passion. When we inquire as to what they mean by passion, the typical response adds to the confusion rather then taking it away. We hear such things as "Well, you know…a desire, a true sense of wanting me…a feeling that I have but they do not…I don't know, just a feeling." Much like the word romantic or the feeling of love, the definition of passion is subjective. So, how can one person tell that the other person is lacking it? We probably can't. We can only know that we feel it or we don't.

Passion is a deep, powerful and overwhelming emotion. It can refer both to sexual feelings and to non-sexual things. We can feel passion, for example, for our hobbies; for music, art, sports, food and wine. And we can kill in the heat of passion! Sexual passion is strong sexual desire, lust or enthusiasm. It is a full expression of sexual energy, free of thought or plan. It is an intense feeling that manifests itself in unbridled, abandoned sexual expression.

Even these definitions feel a bit vague. Therefore, we recommend that you turn to the table of contents of this book and look at the titles of all the CPRs. It may be difficult to define exactly what passion is, but it is our opinion, based on years of experience as therapists, that if you treat your partner in the ways suggested by the titles of the CPRs, you will be able to resuscitate the passion in your relationship or even experience it for the first time!

C P R:

If you are the one feeling that your partner lacks passion, tell your partner how you feel. Try doing this with out blaming or shaming. Taking ownership of your feelings can help. Saying something as simple as, "You know, I just don't feel passion from you," can do it. The issue might easily be resolved if you ask your partner, "Do you feel any passion for me?" You might be surprised when they state, "Yes, of course I do!"

For some, this might be enough. For others, hearing that your partner feels passion is not enough. In that case try telling your partner what you think might help you feel the passion they report having for you. For example, "Well, I'm glad you feel it. But I guess I need something else from you to really feel passion from you." You might make a suggestion: "Would you please try making sounds when we have sex?" or "Would you initiate sex more often?" Of course, there are many different things you might request from your partner depending on what you feel is missing. Be as specific as you can.

Write down three things your partner could do that might help you feel they have passion for you.

1. _____

2. _____

3. _____

Share these things and give your partner a chance to try them.

Of course, if your partner reports a true lack of passion for you, then you both need to identify what is wrong and find ways to solve it. Referring back to the checkup and checklist at the beginning of this book, and trying many of the CPRs offered throughout, will also help tremendously. If these suggestions do not work for you, we recommend that you seek the help of a therapist who can help you dig deeper into the reasons behind the lack of passion.

PATIENCE

People change and grow at different paces. You or your partner might be the type of person who is slow or resistant to change. It's easy to get frustrated, disappointed and angry by seemingly snail-like progress. Many of us want instant gratification. We would like to do a CPR and have it solve all our problems! Unfortunately, relationships are not that simple. Permanent changes in relationships take time to evolve, as they entail letting go of our old, familiar behaviors and taking on new, unfamiliar and often difficult ones. You may, therefore, have many starts and stops and stumbles in your efforts. If your sex life or relationship has been stagnant for many months or years, change will require commitment and patience on your part. It seldom helps to show impatience about your own progress, or to push your partner to do things at your pace. Partners tend to feel pressured and resentful by this and often give up trying.

Remember that positive change in a relationship takes time, but if you are persistent, it will usually pay off. Consider using Thomas Edison as your role model. It took him 300 tries to perfect the light bulb! His positive philosophy was that being patient allowed him to achieve his desired goal. He said, "He that can have patience can have what he will". Nor was he discouraged by the number of attempts it took to achieve his goal. He said, "If I find 10,000 ways something won't work, I haven't failed. I am not discouraged, because every wrong attempt discarded is often a step forward." So, for example, if you try a certain sexual position and you are uncomfortable in it, then you know that is the wrong position for you. That's a step forward! Try another and another until you find one that feels good to you.

C P R:

The solution here is to relax and not be in a hurry. Note some of the steps that your partner has taken to try to enrich your relationship, and reflect on the effort that's been made. The important thing to remember is that each new thing (however seemingly small or hard-earned) that you incorporate into your relationship will positively change the dynamics of the relationship. Rather than impatiently focusing on how slowly things are moving or on all the things that are still lacking in your sex life, focus instead on the efforts that you and your partner have made (however slow) to better the relationship and let each other know how happy and appreciative you are for the growth and change that is there.

Jot down three things that your partner has recently done in an effort to resolve your intimate and sexual problems, regardless of the outcome. Reflect on them and offer your partner some appreciation for each one.

1. _____

2. _____

3. _____

PEACEFULNESS

Although this book is geared towards couples who love each other, it is not unusual for some of these couples to be involved in a power struggle. One or both partners, either due to insecurity, a competitive nature or unresolved resentment, have a need to "win". You don't need to be a genius to know that in the majority of relationships where there is constant bickering and arguments, the sex life is going to be non-existent or bad. How can we possibly want to be intimate with someone who demeans us or does not respect our acts, thoughts or decisions?

Yes, some people have marvelous "make-up" sex after an argument. Make-up sex can intensify sexual desire and pleasure as long as the fights are not extreme and don't occur on a regular basis. If arguments happen frequently, however, then the tendency is to distance ourselves emotionally and physically from our partners. Yet, some people find the need to be in control and "right" in every situation and will fight for it. They would rather be right than be in a peaceful and happy relationship. They may win the battle but they lose the war. Peaceful, nurturing relationships, on the other, hand tend to enhance desire, passion and intimacy.

C P R:

C
P
R

Of course it would be great to stop fighting altogether. However, that may not be realistic and, in fact, it may be healthy to have a bit of fighting now and then. Therefore, if the way the two of you fight and the frequency of your fights, leave one or both of you feeling wounded, angry or distant, then you may want to learn methods to make your fighting less frequent and more productive.

There are literally hundreds of communication models out there designed specifically to help couples live more peacefully together. Why so many? Because different couples respond better to different methods and writers have different ways of saying basically the same things. While researching and learning different communication models may be helpful in your case, most readers will find that the wide variety of methods all boil down to some very common, easily identifiable and easy to utilize concepts, including such things as assuring that the fighting is fair, safe and time limited.

Remember that this book is designed to help you work together, in good faith, to solve your relationship and sexual problems. So keep this in mind and sit down together when you are both in a fairly good and cooperative mood. Separately, write down ways that the two of you breech fairness in your fighting, just like Mary and Bob did here:

Mary wrote:

1. I compare Bob to his father while we fight.

2. I attack Bob's manliness during fights which have nothing to do with his being a man.

3. I remind Bob of things I don't like about him that have nothing to do with the issue we are fighting about at the moment.

Bob wrote:

1. I swear and call Mary names when we fight.

2. I throw things and get very loud.

3. I threaten to leave and never come back, even when we're fighting over small things.

Ways I hit below the belt when fighting with my partner:

1. _____

2. _____

3. _____

Ways my partner hits below the belt when fighting:

1. _____

2. _____

3. _____

Now discuss these issues together and make a pact to avoid bringing these harmful below the belt issues into your fights. Write down five common agreements you make, such as "we agree to leave each other's parents out of our fights", or "we agree to never get loud enough for the neighbors to hear us fighting".

1. _____

2. _____

3. _____

4. _____

5. _____

Pull out this page and remind each other of it next time you find yourselves fighting. An even better solution is to try to review this agreement in advance, if you can see a fight coming. This will likely help you have a fairer and more productive fight. Be sure to also limit the time you fight. Twenty minutes should be enough. After that, you will probably circle through the same old stuff and find neither of you are listening to the other person any more. Finally, we strongly recommend you do what Mary and Bob agreed to do to create a more peaceful relationship, namely: NEVER FIGHT IN THE BEDROOM! Make sure that the bedroom is reserved for sleeping and lovemaking, not fighting!

C

P

R

PEEL

When we see our partner naked for the first time, we typically get sexually excited. The novelty of seeing that person in the nude can be profound. The desire for sex can be very strong. However, like anything else, seeing our partner naked day after day, month after month, year after year, whether it is in the shower, a hot tub or in bed, can become somewhat routine and boring. Peeling can add some excitement to the situation. It builds anticipation to enjoy the "fruit" inside! After all, we salivate as we peel away the outer layer of an orange, enticed by the color, aroma and texture.

C P R:

Start by asking your partner if you may "peel" them. When given permission, undress your partner very slowly. Take time with each button, clasp or zipper. Feel and smell the fabrics as you strip away each layer. Look carefully at what you expose. A taste here or there can also add to the experience. Notice how the anticipation builds as you get closer and closer to your fully "unpeeled" partner. You may also want to peel off your own clothes and perform a slow, sensuous striptease for your partner.

If you feel uncomfortable with the thought of your partner seeing your naked body, slowly ease into this CPR exercise. First, share your concerns with your partner. He or she will probably reassure you and take some of the pressure off you. Then, when ready, do this CPR in tiny stages, which we call the "peek-a-boo" technique. Rather than taking off your garments and exposing your genitals, breasts or other body parts that you are uncomfortable revealing, instead expose these parts for only a second or two and then cover them up. Go back and forth between brief exposure and cover-up, lengthening the time of exposure until you develop comfort with your partner seeing your naked body and with "peeling".

C
P
R

PERFORMANCE ANXIETY

Performance anxiety refers to worries and expectations that intrude during sex concerning our body or our sexual functioning. When present, it can create serious difficulties with sexual desire, male erections and female orgasms. This anxiety is rooted in societal teachings. Most men believe that to be a good lover they must always be in the mood for sex, always have a firm erection, last long enough to satisfy their partners and be an expert at doing exactly that. Women believe that they must have large breasts, be quickly and noisily responsive and always reach orgasm, or they are failures as sex partners.

This kind of thinking puts a lot of pressure to perform on both partners – but especially men. These thoughts often intrude during sexual activity and create anxiety. We become observers, commentators and graders of our bodies and our sexual functioning rather than being fully involved participants in the act of sex. We criticize ourselves with thoughts like, "my recent weight gain must be a turnoff to my partner," "I'm coming too fast/slowly," "I don't think I'm going to come," "my erection isn't as hard as it should be," or "I don't think that I'm pleasing my partner."

These worries create a self-perpetuating scenario in which the more we worry, the worse we perform. If our thoughts are consumed with worry, then it is difficult, if not impossible, for us to relax enough for us to experience the wonderful sensations that our body receives. This, in turn, leads to a decrease in looking forward to sex, which leads back to the anxiety, which leads back to the poor performance. The self-defeating loop goes on and on.

C P R:

During sensual or sexual activity, stop thinking about anything except what your body is feeling. Focus fully on your body's sensations. To do this, try "mind talk," a focused internal awareness of what is happening, similar to the play-by-play technique used by a sports announcer describing a game. For example, "Her head is on my belly; now she's stroking my penis; her hand is moving up and down my shaft; her grip is strong. It feels wonderful" or "His hand are moving down my body; now he's caressing my stomach in slow circles; his touch feels so soft and gentle; now he's moved down to my thighs; I feel tingly."

Practice the mind talk technique while stroking your partner's face, head, hands and feet or while you are being stroked. Later, when more sexual parts are touched, do the same thing again. Focus on the sensations. Mind talk will keep you in the moment, undistracted and fully engaged in your partner and your pleasure.

Write down three sentences of this kind and practice saying them yourself. That way mind talk will come easier when you are in the real situation.

1. _____

2. _____

3. _____

PERMISSION

Many of us have dull sex lives because we put judgments on certain sexual behaviors and don't permit ourselves to experiment and try them. We stay stuck in old patterns that wear thin with time. We restrict ourselves not only by our judgments but by those of our culture. Lets face it, the world is full of "shoulds" and "should nots." Many of us grew up learning that "nice girls should not enjoy sex" and that "men should be sex experts." To please our partner, we "should" do this or do that. Trying to get it "right" and "perform properly" may have left you feeling that you have little choice. But you do! You can make your sex life what you want it to be as long as you give yourself permission to do so.

What you permit yourself to do will vary greatly from person to person. The most common issues our clients ask permission for, or confirmation of, are things such as masturbation, fantasizing, sharing fantasies with one's partner, cross-dressing, oral sex, anal sex, bondage, domination and discipline.

Many worry, however, that the sexual activities that they want (or don't want), or the frequency in which they engage in sex (or want to), is not normal. We assure you that there is a wide range of human sexual behavior. Normal is whatever is right for the couple (as long as nobody is being hurt or coerced into anything). In fact, you may want to replace the term "normal" with "average" or "common" instead. For example, if the "average" person enjoys pizza and you don't, so what? There is no morality attached to this. It is not good or bad, right or wrong. The same concept applies where sexual behavior and frequency is concerned. It doesn't matter what the people next door do or how often they do it! This is not a competition. What matters is that you do what feels comfortable to you and your partner, and with a frequency that satisfies the two of you.

C P R:

Make a list below of three things you would like to give yourself permission to explore. For each item, write down the reasons why you have not yet done those things. Next, write down reasons to try these yet to be explored activities.

For example:

Jack wrote: "I'd like to give myself permission to spank Jill, but I'm afraid that I'll hurt her or even, over time, that it might turn me into a violent person. I've read books that assure me that I will not become violent and Jill says that being spanked is a turnon for her, so I would like to try to do it if she will guide me slowly and we talk a lot about what's going on."

1. _____

2. _____

3. _____

Now pick one from the list that would be the easiest and most comfortable for you. Try the activity and be sure to give yourself credit for stretching beyond your comfort zone. For example, if you decided to masturbate, pick a time and a place when you are sure you will be alone and uninterrupted. If the activity involves a partner, share your thoughts and feelings about it with them and seek their cooperation.

Please be assured, however, that self-permission goes two ways. Not only do we encourage you to give yourself permission to try certain sexual behaviors but also encourage you to give yourself permission to freely, without guilt, say "no" to engaging behaviors that are morally or physically repugnant to you.

If you are the partner of the person saying "no", do not push or coerce that person into doing something that they are not ready or willing to do. Instead, be understanding and give them time. Perhaps as you work through this book and your partner experiences more comfort and intimacy in the relationship, and the two of you are communicating and treating each other in special ways, your partner will feel more open to trying what you request.

PERSEVERANCE

Okay, so you may be feeling hopeless at this point. You've been working on the CPRs for weeks, or months, and things still don't seem better. You may feel like giving up, but don't! There is no correct time span for working through this book. It is not unusual to take a year, or more, for some couples to methodically do all of the CPR exercises and deal with their intimacy issues. If you give up, you are giving up on bettering your relationship and your sex life. However difficult going forward may seem, if you don't persevere you will likely be back to where you were before your started reading this book. In fact, you might even be in a worse situation than before if your partner is resentful of your lack of perseverance.

C P R:

As you've done before in this book, once again note any progress or positive changes that you two have made. Write two of them down now.

1. _____

2. _____

Next, express your concerns about your lack of progress to your partner. If your partner is feeling more positive than you, this conversation may be all you need to feel back on track. If they are also feeling a lack of progress, then go back to the beginning of the book and review page by page both the progress made and any areas where you might have treated the CPR suggestions too lightly. Try doing some of the previous CPR suggestions again and then continue on from there.

PETS

Pets generally bring great pleasure to individuals. Having a pet can also add pleasure to a couple's life as they get to share the joy of raising a little loved one, especially if they do not have children. Many things pets do, and many things we do with our pets, are both fun and can contribute much to a couple's shared experience in life.

At the same time, having pets may hinder our romantic and sexual connection. People frequently love their pets so much that they express more love to them than to their partner. The dog or cat may also sleep between the couple and interfere when they are trying to have sex. Some pets have been known to be so possessive of their owner that it leads the owner to having to choose between their pet and their partner, new lover or potential life partner.

C P R:

Think of the ways you speak to and touch your pet(s). Pay close attention to what you give them that you are not giving your partner. Make sure you offer your partner the same kind of affection at least once a day, preferably before you offer the same to your pet.

If a dog or cat is in the habit of sleeping between you in bed, reconsider this privilege you are giving them. Perhaps they need to be given their own sleeping area. You may also try scheduling lovemaking sessions for times when your pet is not likely to be on the bed, or put the pet in another room and close the door to your bedroom while you are being sexually intimate with your partner.

If you have an overly possessive pet that will not accept your partner's presence, contact a professional pet behaviorist. They can find systematic ways to deal with your pet's jealousy.

C

P

R

PETTING

Most women – and yes, most men – report that sex just isn't very good if they are not aroused. It can hurt if our bodies are not properly ready for certain sexual activities. For example, vaginal intercourse can be painful if the woman's vagina is not moist and the cervix has not moved up and out of the way. Similarly, a man's penis can feel pain if fondled and yanked when not sufficiently hard enough. Without some form of preparation, a lack of desire for sex may exist. Furthermore, many people, but especially women, find sex to be unsatisfactory if it does not start with some kind of emotional bonding.

Partners who are new to each other have increased risks when it comes to sex. Nowadays, sex can be downright dangerous. In addition, new couples may need time to get into sync with each other's bodies and sexual preferences. Petting, which entails touching your partner with their clothes on, or with a hand under the clothes, can alleviate many problems. This kind of touch typically feels good and arousing. It includes stroking and rubbing and may even lead to orgasm. In our dating days, petting is often our first exquisite taste of couple sexual relating. It can help put us in the mood, prepare our bodies for sexual activities, and is what sex therapists call one of the safest sex practices.

C P R:

Pretend that you are both teens on a date and neither one of you feels ready to engage in intercourse. Have a "make out" session with your partner instead. See how excited you can get kissing and touching with your clothes on. If you are spending the night together, following your petting session and before getting into bed, try doing a non-sexual activity, such as watching TV or playing a board game so as to separate the two. This will lead to a greater appreciation for what petting is and how it feels.

C

P

R

PHOBIAS, ANXIETIES & INHIBITIONS

Sexual phobias, anxieties and inhibitions can greatly interfere with joyous sexual functioning. They can come from prior sexual assault or trauma, or from early learning that defines certain sexual acts as taboo or perverted. The fears or inhibitions that arise from these experiences or teachings are imprinted in our brains and interfere even when we are with a partner that we love. Frequently, it's not that we don't trust our partners, but rather that we feel panic, anxiety or disgust with these activities. One solution is to slowly desensitize ourselves from our negative reactions.

C P R:

On a piece of paper, make a column on the left, numbered 0-100 in increments of 10. Next, picture a scene that gives you a sense of peace and calm. Write that beside the zero. Write the anxiety-provoking or feared activity beside the number 100. The other spaces are to be filled with scenes that gradually intensify your discomfort, starting at 10 and moving up to 90, although it is not necessary to have every number between 0-100 filled in.

C
P
R

	JILL'S ANXIETY LADDER		*JACK'S ANXIETY LADDER*
100	penile penetration	*100*	performing cunnilingus
90	Jack in position to penetrate	*90*	smelling Jill's genitals
80	Jack is fully erect	*80*	my head between Jill's legs
70	Jack stimulates my genitals	*70*	moving my head down her body
60	Jack plays with my body	*60*	Jill asks me to go down on her
50	Jack plays with my breasts	*50*	Jill going down on me
40	Jack begins undressing me	*40*	sucking Jill's breasts
30	the kissing becomes passionate	*30*	making out with Jill
20	Jack begins kissing me	*20*	cuddling with Jill
10	Jack sitting by ocean with me	*10*	slow dancing with Jill
0	sitting by the ocean	*0*	talking with Jill

Now create your own anxiety ladder. Give this a lot of thought. If you don't have anxiety about any sexual behavior, chose to desensitize yourself to something sexual that you've been shy or hesitant to try.

PARTNER I – ANXIETY LADDER	PARTNER II – ANXIETY LADDER
100	100
90	90
80	80
70	70
60	60
50	50
40	40
30	30
20	20
10	10
0	0

C

P

R

Once you've created your anxiety ladder, begin working with it: put yourself in a relaxing position and visualize the zero scene. If it does not bring up any anxiety, move on to the 10 scene. Whenever you reach a number that evokes even a little anxiety, return to zero, calm yourself and then go back and again picture the anxiety-provoking scene. Go back and forth until you no longer experience anxiety. Repeat this format for all the numbers.

The anxiety ladder, based on the work of Dr. Debora Phillips, is an effective desensitization exercise for many (but certainly not all) people. Some have highly developed visualization skills and others do not. If the latter is the case for you, you might instead try to debate away your anxiety. For instance, write your objections to a certain activity on one side of the page and write counter-arguments to them on the other side in the hope that your intellect will cancel out your anxieties.

If going through the anxiety ladder or debating of your objections, does not desensitize you to the anxiety that certain sexual acts provoke in you, you might consider seeking the help of a therapist.

PILLOW TALK

Couples frequently tell us that they feel disconnected with each other at the end of making love. They lie in bed wondering how "it was" for their partner and what their partner is thinking. Couples also complain that they never get a chance to talk with each other about things other than necessities. Pillow talk addresses both of these issues.

Pillow talk refers to conversation that you may have following a sexual encounter. Pillow talk can be an intimate and sweet time as you bathe in the afterglow of a positive sexual encounter. It is a beautiful extension to your lovemaking, and provides a loving alternative to simply rolling over and going to sleep. Pillow talk can also be helpful before a sexual encounter. Many couples find that lying on the bed and talking helps them to make a powerful initial emotional bond prior to any sexual contact.

C P R:

Agree before you start a sexual encounter that you will try pillow talk at the end. That way, neither of you will be caught off guard. When you mutually agree that you've reached that "after sex" time, hold each other or turn and look at each other. Lightly stroke and fondle each other as you transition into a verbal exchange. It may be a wonderful time to talk about the positive aspects of your sexual encounter and how good you feel. Talk with each other for at least three minutes the first time. Partners are soft and vulnerable at this time and are more willing to hear you.

Before your next session of Pillow Talk, write down three positive comments that you would like to share with your partner about their lovemaking.

1. _____

2. _____

3. _____

Write down any topic(s) that you would like to discuss during pillow talk time.

1. _____

2. _____

3. _____

PLAN

Planning sex feels uncomfortable to many. After all, isn't sex supposed to be spontaneous? The reality is that it very seldom is. Americans are working longer and harder. We have computers, PDAs, faxes, cell phones and pagers designed to save us time but which instead leash us to our work and electronic devices. Add in the kids, pets, in-laws, hobbies and household chores and who has time to be spontaneous? Who has quality time for couple intimacy?

There can be spontaneity with sex and time for sex if you plan for it. Planning makes a place for sex in our busy, overscheduled lives. In fact, it builds anticipation – and with anticipation comes excitement. For example, imagine you want to go on a picnic. To do so, you plan a date, a time, a location, a meal to take and something to sit on. Between the planning and the day of the picnic, you most likely will find yourself getting excited and looking forward to it. Once you get there, you are free to let yourself go and be spontaneous. Planned sex can be the same way.

Planning sensual and sexual activities allows you to get chores completed, be groomed and get yourself into a sexual mindset. A planned sexual encounter is also beneficial in eliminating the likelihood of rejection for the partner who typically initiates. It is a time that you both chose together in advance and that you can count on.

C P R:

Schedule a date for sensuality, and later, when ready, for sex. Once you have scheduled your date, assess what you feel you need and want so that you can look forward to and enjoy sensual and/or sexual contact. Do you need to take some form of birth control with you? Music? Massage lotion? When you make plans and follow through on them, it shows respect and caring for your partner and your relationship. Without planning, it's too easy to let your kids, work or chores ruin the fun.

Write down three things you feel you need or want in order to be able to enjoy the planned sex you have scheduled.

1. _____

2. _____

3. _____

C

P

R

PLAY

Children have a natural proclivity toward play and an enormous capacity for it. Sadly, by the time we reach adulthood many of us have lost that playfulness. There is no time to play. We are engrossed in jobs, kids and household responsibilities. And even when we do play, it is generally competitive rather than just for plain fun. This same sense of seriousness is often carried into the bedroom.

Many of us take sex too seriously. Rather than viewing sex as something playful and enjoyable, we often see it as an obligation or a chore, with a series of steps that must be done in a certain order, for a certain length of time and with a definite goal in mind. This puts undue pressure on one or both partners. Even the word foreplay is not real play. It is goal-oriented play. It consists of activities engaged in mainly for the purpose of creating the sexual arousal necessary for penetration and orgasm rather than being play for its own sake – namely, play whose only purpose is to create enjoyment, happiness and intimacy.

C P R:

Start a sexual contact by agreeing that the idea is to play and do nothing else and see what happens. If the man gets and then loses an erection, it's okay. It's not a requirement for play. With no goal, orgasm is not required. If it happens great! But don't work toward it.

Some examples of play activities are:

- *Paint your partner using edible items such as chocolate sauce and whipped cream. Afterward, lick off the art and enjoy more pleasure.*
- *Perform a striptease for your partner.*
- *Buy some sex toys and explore them together.*
- *Go to a bar and pretend you don't know each other. Pick each other up and go home together for a one-night stand.*
- *Purchase a sex board game and play it.*
- *Have a naked pillow fight.*
- *Explore each other's bodies using only feathers.*
- *Do a lap dance for your partner.*
- *Take a bubble bath together and play in the water.*
- *Take a shower together and slide against each other's soapy bodies.*
- *Squirt each other with water pistols.*
- *Feed each other.*
- *Do some or all of the above play activities or make up your own.*

Discuss possible play activities with your partner right now. The choice is endless. Agree on three that the two of you are willing to try and write them down here. Be sure to try them soon!

1. _____

2. _____

3. _____

PLEASE

Most of us really want to please our partners, both in general and in a sexual way. You may be reading this book because your partner said "you don't please me," and you've decided you want to learn how. You may have forgotten or never known how to please your partner. Your partner may have changed to the point in which you no longer know what will please them. Or you may have decided you did not want to please your partner, out of anger, frustration or other reasons, and now you've decided you want to. Frequently partners in long-term relations also "forget" to use the word "please" and assume its okay to touch, grab, and fondle the other without asking first. Either way, the lack of pleasing or requesting can lead to great distance and mistrust in a relationship. And don't forget to thank your partner when they are trying to please you!

C P R:

If you truly want to please your partner, then don't guess what to do. Find out exactly what it takes. Instead of approaching your partner in your usual way, learn to please them in their preferred way. You might say: "I really want to please you. Is there something I can do for you or to you?" If your partner gives you a specific request that's acceptable to you, then say "with pleasure" and fulfill it! Nothing shows a person that their partner really wants to please them more than having what they asked for done for them in a gracious and loving way!

If you are having a rough time thinking of pleasing your partner because you have underlying feelings of resentment for them, perhaps it will help you to focus on a philosophy of the Marriage Encounter movement. Their credo is: "Love is a daily decision". They say that it's easy to love and please your partner when everything is going smoothly but that we tend to withhold love when things are rough, They ask that you wake up each day and make a conscious decision to nurture, love and please your partner, even when your partner or relationship is not the way you would like them to be. If you both can follow through on this, over time, you will feel better about both yourselves and your partner, and your relationship and your sex life should improve tremendously.

List three things that your partner can do to please you, and share that list with them.

1. _____

2. _____

3. _____

PRACTICE

Many people falsely believe that everything sexual should come naturally, without any education or practice. Some feel like inferior lovers if they have to learn how to touch their partner in a certain way or learn new sexual behaviors. And yet how else would they know with certainty how to sexually please their partner? We grew up in a society that didn't provide us with progressive and comprehensive sex education; instead, it supplied double messages, unrealistic expectations and prohibitions that left us confused and anxious with regard to sex. The only way for sex or any skill to flow naturally is through learning and then lots of practice.

C P R:

Practice makes perfect. Doing something once is not going to fix the problem, especially if you have to undo prior negative sexual learning, nor is it going to help you learn how to please your partner. The CPRs in this book need to be done at least three times. The first time that you do a specific CPR, you may be nervous and spend the time worrying. The second time, you may be more relaxed but still feel that you are in uncharted territory. The more you do the CPRs that you want to add to your sexual repertoire, the more skilled you will become at doing them and the more knowledgeable and relaxed you will feel. Go through the book and pick out three CPRs you've already done that you are interested in doing better.

Write them down here and practice at least one within the next 24 hours!

1. _____

2. _____

3. _____

PREFERENCE

By the time most of us have been in a relationship or dating for a couple of years, we develop what becomes our technique, our approach to lovemaking. We become comfortable, or comfortable enough, with a certain style of initiating sex, kissing, stroking and the like. We continue this approach through subsequent relationships assuming that "one style fits all." Within an existing relationship, we believe that if it worked once, it will always work. Sometimes our preferred approach works for us but not for our partner. They may have a different preference. The difference can cause great dissatisfaction for you both. We all want to be skilled lovers. Learning to love our partners in their preferred way can lead to great satisfaction for both partners and will make us great lovers in our partner's eyes.

C P R:

Write down your vision of ideal sex, a whole scenario from beginning to end. Be sure to include time of day, setting, type of music if any, clothing, who initiates and how, what is said and done and how long it lasts.

Compare your preferred vision with your partner's. Take turns living out each other's scenarios, unless there is something your partner wants that is so distasteful to you that you can't consider trying it – in which case, modify the script. See if you can combine elements of both partners' preferred sex scene into one pleasurable experience for both. For example, one partner might prefer to have sex at night in the shower. The other might prefer to have sex in bed in the morning. Combining elements of both, a compromise might be, "We take a shower together, play with each other's soapy bodies, dry each other off and then have intercourse on the bed. We'll do this sometimes in the morning and sometimes in the evening."

Write your preferred sex scenario in detail:

_____

_____

After sharing your ideal sex scene with your partner, write a new one that encompasses elements from both of your scripts:

_____

_____

_____

Sometimes act out your script; at other times act out your partner's script: and at yet other times act out your combined compromise script. This will add variety to your practices as well as increase communication between you.

PRETENDING

Some of you are reading this book because your sex life is dead. Others are reading it because of a crisis such as an affair or other violation of the relationship. If the latter is the case, then at this point of the book you might also have found that the crisis is resolved, at least for the moment, and motivation to continue trying is waning. Some of you might not have experienced a crisis and are still struggling with that initial lack of motivation. Regardless, it's time to increase the efforts or keep the excellent pace of progress growing. Many people find pretending a helpful tool in achieving this goal.

C P R:

Don't take your partner's love for granted. Treat them as if you were to lose them at any moment. Pretend that you just heard "I want a divorce if things don't improve," or that you just discovered your partner is having an affair and desperately want to win them back. Immerse yourself in the fantasy and do whatever you might do in reality to win your partner. Or try pretending that your partner is dying of a terrible disease or is going off to war soon, that you might not see them again, and that you want to make the last few weeks together as happy as they can be.

This pretending assignment has the best results if your partner is unaware that your actions are a response to a fear-based fantasy. All they know is that the loving attention that they are getting feels wonderful and makes them feel special and more loving and appreciative of you.

As a result of pretending you are about to lose your loved one, write three things you will do this week to "save" the relationship, or to do "before it's too late."

1. _____

2. _____

3. _____

PRIME TIME

Did you know that some times are better than others for making love? Yes, it's true! Poor timing for sex can ruin the moment and lead to frustration, disappointment and anger. You can imagine that during an illness or stressful times certain people cannot even think of having sex, while for others, sex is the release that they need to help them cope with hard times.

Daily and monthly prime times vary for different people and between the sexes. Prime time for women frequently occurs within the few days just prior to the beginning of their periods and in the middle of their cycle when they are ovulating. Prime time for a woman often may also require having life's daily demands cleared and in order – having children bathed and in bed and chores out of the way so that she is free to relax and enjoy her partner.

For men, daily cycles are more important. Most men find their prime time is somewhere early in the morning, the time of day when their testosterone is at its highest level. Of course your body may be different than others. Many men also find sex is a release that helps them relax at the end of a day, while women often require relaxation first in order to feel ready for sex.

C P R:

C
P
R

Discover your own prime time first. Do this by keeping a calendar for two or more months and monitor the times when you are most in the mood and when you are not. Is it related to your menstrual cycle, a certain time of the week, a certain time of the day? At the end of the two months, compare notes with your partner and find those times when there are fairly good matches. Making love during just these special times may be more rewarding for you than all the other times that are not prime time. It may be so good, in fact, that you might decide to only make love during those times and skip the rest. A few great sessions of lovemaking may be far superior to tons of lousy sessions fraught with boredom and frustration.

If no match is found, however, make a date for sex at a time that works well for one partner. The other partner, with the advance knowledge of when the next sexual encounter will take place, can prepare by taking a relaxing bath, reading something romantic or erotic, having a glass of wine or whatever they find helpful to create a prime time sexual experience.

Write down your initial guess as to when your prime time might be and when that might be for your partner.

My prime time probably is:

_____

My partner's prime time probably is:

_____

After the monitoring period, come back to this page and write down the results.

My actual prime time is:

_____

My partner's actual prime time is:

_____

PRIORITIZE

Most of the people we see for sex therapy are overly involved in everything except their sexual relationship. They find time for shopping, sports, kids, friends, work, the Internet and social events, but not for sex. Many report being too tired for sex at the end of the day and yet never make time for sex during the day, or even on weekends.

In the early stages of your relationship you most likely kept your job, friends, family and exercise routine and still managed to spend plenty of time to be with your newfound love. Your new partner was a priority. After all, could you have built a healthy and happy relationship without taking the time to focus on them?

C P R:

It may seem like an artificial suggestion, but schedule your intimacy! Sit down together right now and schedule at least one appointment per week for the next month and pencil it in below. Consider these appointments a form of relationship maintenance or rebuilding and give them the same importance that you would give a medical or dental appointment.

Look at what you are willing to give up in your current daily fixed routine to create time for intimacy and make that change. It may feel like a sacrifice to give up certain activities, but you have been sacrificing a great deal more by not being sensually or sexually intimate with each other. Decide right now that intimacy with your partner is just as important as your work, your children and your other commitments, if not more so. Make your sex life a priority now!

List what you are willing to give up from your routine so that you have more time for your partner and for intimacy.

1. _____

2. _____

3. _____

C
P
R

PROFESSIONALS (THERAPISTS)

The various CPRs in this book are designed for couples to try on their own, with room to adjust for personal tastes and values. If your overall relationship with each other is stable and strong, doing the CPRs in this book may be sufficient to revitalize your sex life. If you find, though, that you are not able to work together on the CPRs, or that major relationship issues are getting in your way, you may need to seek professional help.

Professional help comes in different forms and some are better than others for confronting different issues. When it comes to sexuality, sex therapists, sex counselors and sexologists (all similar professionals with many overlapping skills and levels of training) are usually the best. However, if drugs, alcohol, abuse issues or mental/emotional illness are underlying the sexual problems, you may need to seek a psychotherapist, typically advertised as a psychologist, marriage and family therapist or clinical social worker, for talk and/or behavioral therapy. A medical doctor (M.D.), preferably a psychiatrist, is required if medications are needed. Many professional sex therapists and sexologists are also licensed as psychotherapists and may be able to assist you with most of your needs. At other times, self-help groups such as Alcoholics Anonymous are the best place to seek the special help one requires.

C P R:

If you think you are going to need professional help, discuss this as a couple. Decide what kind of help is most appropriate for your situation. Once you have made that decision, ask a trusted friend, family member or physician for a referral. Phone books and local newspapers may also lead you to the right person.

Unfortunately, most phone books lack categories for sex therapists or sexologists. To find them, you might have to look under psychotherapy, marriage and family therapists, or psychologists. Nowadays searching Web sites usually bears the greatest fruit. Also try AASECT (the American Association of Sexuality Educators, Counselors and Therapists) at www.aasect.org, or the American College of Sexology site at www.sexologist.org, to find a sex therapist in your area. Or try searching for local associations of therapists and/or self-help groups. Either way, keep in mind that you have a right (that professionals respect) to shop around and find the best fit for you.

Write down the names and phone numbers of three therapists who work with sexual issues. Do this even if you don't think at this time that you will need them. It will help tremendously should the situation suddenly change.

1. _____

2. _____

3. _____

PROHIBIITON

Certain intimate and sexual activities may be very uncomfortable for one or both of you. Just the thought of "it" may be enough to kill your sexual desire. Couples frequently agree, verbally or not, to avoid things such as using sexual slang or engaging in anal intercourse, because they both find it to be distasteful. Other times, one partner will avoid all intimate and sexual activities out of fear that their partner will then expect or demand the one activity the person wishes to avoid the most. The more we feel sexual pressure, the more we typically pull away and avoid sexual contact as much as possible.

Requested prohibitions that you both agreee to comply with can add clarity and safety to sexual activities. For example, if you're feeling pressured to have oral sex, agree to prohibit or ban it temporarily. This may greatly enhance your ability to give and receive other romantic or sexual gestures because you will know that the thing that is making you uneasy (i.e. oral sex) is off-limits for the moment. For those who have been sexually abused in the past, a prohibition may be long-term, continuing until you reach a point where your trust is restored and your comfort level is achieved. Abiding by the prohibition agreement can also positively change the dynamics in your relationship. It shows that you respect your partner's feelings and can be patient, knowing you are investing in a future of better sex. When you are both clear on what is prohibited, then you may proceed to do anything else that is comfortable and mutually pleasing.

C P R:

Start a sexual encounter by first asking each other "what are your rules this time?" Noting that the rules may and will change is important as it adds clarity and safety to your sexual interactions..

List any sexual activities that you would temporarily like to prohibit. Communicate this to your partner and make an agreement to check with each other monthly as to whether or not to continue the prohibition.

1. _____

2. _____

3. _____

PROLONG

Many women, and some men, complain that foreplay is too short and that their partner rushes to the "real sex." What they mean by this is that they spend too little time enjoying sexual activities other than intercourse. Much pleasure, and some specific sensations, in these other activities are missed. In addition, many report an inability to reach orgasm when they are rushed to intercourse.

"Quickies" can be fine in times when a partner is swept away with desire, but as a rule, the buildup that comes from prolonging sensual and sexual activities greatly heightens pleasure and arousal. When, for example, kissing or simple touch is prolonged, we may feel new, pleasurable sensations that we did not feel previously because they required time to emerge. Prolonging touch also relays the message that you really care and are involved in what you are doing, rather than rushing to get it over with so that you can move on to something else.

C P R:

By now you have discovered many parts of your partner's body that they find pleasurable to have touched. Try touching some of these parts again, but this time, take twice as long as you did the last time. In other words, prolong the experience.

When you think you've spent enough time on a specific part, continue for another two minutes. Again, not rushing toward the "finish line" may be difficult for some of you, but it usually pays off for both partners. Use the same prolonging behavior for any intimate or sexual activity, such as eye gazing, hand holding, kissing or fondling. See if that feels any different and ask your partner what the extra time does for them.

C

P

R

PROSE AND POETRY

Words of endearment and poetic declarations of love are frequently missing in long-term relationships, and this lack can contribute to the death of a sex life. Over the years, many of us become complacent or full of resentment, and verbal kindnesses fall by the wayside. If it's been months, or even years, since you've spoken words of love to your partner, you may find it difficult to summon up those words.

The written word can be extremely helpful in these cases. Reading printed words aloud is less threatening and easier to do than spontaneously coming up with them on your own. Reading prose and poetry is a romantic and seductive activity couples can share together. For example, some find it arousing to read poetry, such as King Solomon's Songs of Songs or Shakespeare's love sonnets. Others respond better to more modern prose such as Eminem's rappings, ballads, Penthouse short stories, or Hallmark love cards. Reading other people's work may also lead you to come up with, and express in written or verbal form, your own original words of love and seduction.

C P R:

Pick some things in print that you find romantic or erotic and read them to each other. Discuss what you've come up with and narrow it down to what you both find pleasing.

Next, try your hand at a poem or write a passionate love letter. Secretly write messages to your loved one and place them somewhere where they find and enjoy it. For example, put love notes in your partner's car windshield, on the bathroom mirror, in their lunch box, in their gym bag or in their shoes. Leave post-its on their nightstand or pillow.

Write an enticing message below right now. When done, read it to your partner and see if they like it. If they don't, find out why and try again.

_____

_____

_____

_____

_____

_____

PUCKER UP

So often we have heard clients say that they are turned-off by poor kissing. Kisses are either too wet or too dry, too hard or too soft, have too much tongue or not enough tongue. Without this level of intimacy and satisfaction, many lose interest in going further with other sexual acts. If they do, they report it feels shallow, uninteresting and boring.

Kissing is important. A kiss is typically the first physical contact we have with our potential partners and may well determine whether or not the relationship will go anywhere. If couples in a relationship stop kissing, they are sacrificing a passion-inducing and intensely intimate part of their lives. Despite what some think, kissing is the most intimate sexual act. Studies have shown that many prostitutes and professional escorts avoid kissing their clients. They save kissing for their own, private relationships, as they see kissing as more intimate than any of the other sexual acts in which they engage. By becoming intimate, they risk losing their objectivity and their ability to do their work.

There are a wide variety of kisses to suit all tastes. Kisses can be playful, affectionate, comforting, healing, passionate and highly arousing or they can be unpleasant. Finding just the right kisses for the two of you will greatly enhance your success in breathing vitality into your sex life.

C P R:

C
P
R

Remember and discuss the way kissing was for you as a couple when you first started dating. Was it enjoyable and exciting or simply tolerable? Share this with your partner and see where you agree. If you liked what you first had, try kissing each other again in the same way for three minutes. Discuss how it feels. Does it still work for you? Would you like something different? If the original kissing was not satisfactory, discuss why.

Next, regardless of whether the original style was satisfactory or not, explore different kinds of kisses with each other, starting with baby kisses all over the face. Then "pucker up" and do light pecks on the lips, increasing the firmness with each attempt. Finally move on to wet kisses and tongue kisses. Whenever you feel discomfort, stop, return to kisses that were comfortable for you and then try again to do the type of kiss that causes you discomfort. You don't have to kiss for long. Just try a few seconds initially.

Discuss your findings and feelings with your partner. If your partner said that your kissing needed improvement and you got angry or offended, remember that the goal is for you to have a passionate couple relationship. Learning to kiss your partner in their preferred way will bring you closer to that goal.

Work your way to the point that you kiss each other passionately every day.

PURR

When a cat purrs, it is signaling that it's feeling good. When we feel good during non-sexual activities, we tend to smile, laugh or squeal out loud. During sexual activities, however, many of us are too inhibited to make pleasure noises. Many of our clients complain that they don't look forward to sex because their partner just "lies there like a piece of wood" during sex, without making any pleasure sounds or movements.

Some of us need intense inner focus during sex and so are silent. Many of us, however, hold back sounds out of fear that it is unladylike or not masculine and that we will scare our partners, be laughed at or be otherwise rejected. Yet making noises can greatly enhance sexual pleasure for us and provides excellent feedback to our partners that they are doing things that give us pleasure.

C P R:

C	
P	
R	

When alone, practice making the noises which you imagine you might make during sex. Exaggerate the panting, moans, groans, sounds and body movements that accompany sex. Don't be self-conscious. Go all out. You are alone so nobody will see or hear you.

Another form of sexual purring to try is verbal messages such as: "I like that; that feels good; umm; oh yes; more; you're a terrific lover." This form of purring can be powerful, since most partners hunger for validation of their lovemaking techniques. And don't forget the perfect statement of intimacy, the "I love you."

Do this exercise a few times while alone. Then during a non-sexual time, try making the noises with your partner, with the two of you purring both individually and together. You may feel silly or awkward making these sounds at first but persevere until you develop comfort with them. Finally, incorporate your purrs into sexual activities, making those rehearsed sounds of pleasure until it feels natural.

Write down three sounds or body movements you would like to become comfortable making during sex.

1. _____

2. _____

3. _____

NOTES:

_____

_____

_____

_____

_____

_____

_____

_____

_____

_____

CHAPTER 4

C
P
R

The R's

REALISM

REASSURE   RECEIVE

REHEARSE   RELAPSE   RELAX

RELIGION   REMEMBER   RENDEVOUZ

RENEW VOWS   RESPECT   RESPONSIBILITY   RITUAL

ROLE PLAY   ROMANCE   ROSE-COLORED GLASSES   ROYAL TREATMENT   RUTS

REALISM

When we dig deeply into the sexual problems that couples share with us, we frequently find that the root of these problems lies in unrealistic expectations. For example, couples commonly believe that good sex must include simultaneous orgasms, that a sexual encounter is a failure if one or both partners "fail" to have an orgasm, that a man must have a full erection, that size matters, that a woman must lubricate freely on her own, that sex should be natural and spontaneous and that "real sex" equals penetration. Hanging on to these expectations typically leads to disillusionment, frustration, anger and distance. We are left feeling that either we, or our partners, are flawed.

The best and most realistic expectation is to find pleasure in being intimate with each other.

C P R:

Examine your own expectations about sex and write them down here:

_____

_____

_____

_____

_____

_____

Now look at these expectations and see whether or not they are realistic and drop any that are not. If you are not sure whether what you expect sexually is realistic, consult a recent sex education book or look up your question on one of the many sex information websites available on the Internet. Discuss your findings with your partner.

REASSURE

You may find your partner complaining that not enough progress is being made in the bedroom and that they are losing confidence and feel like quitting. Perhaps your partner expects that your romance or sex life should have changed much faster than it has – perhaps the dates are not happening or the efforts to be romantic seem to miss the mark. Your partner may even feel that they are carrying the load by themselves. They need reassurance from you. Reassurance works as a motivator to continue working with the CPR program, and helps you feel as if you are working as a team.

C P R:

Listen to your partner's concerns and acknowledge their feelings. Let them know that you understand how they feel. Remind yourself and your partner what life was like before you started this book, and agree that quitting now would be self-defeating. Restore confidence by acknowledging the efforts you and your partner have already made and the progress you see. Reassure your partner that you love them, that they and the relationship are important to you and that you plan to be there for the long run.

List three reassuring statements that you can give to your partner.

1. _____

2. _____

3. _____

RECEIVE

Some people are active receivers during sensual and sexual activity while others are passive receivers. The active receiver is one who takes pleasure in having their partner do things to them that they themselves request and enjoy. They supply verbal and physical feedback, letting the giver know what feels good and what does not.

The passive receiver, on the other hand, is silent. They submit to whatever the giver chooses, ask for nothing and provide no feedback. Some of these clients report that they can't relax unless they are doing something to please their partner at the same time that they are receiving. Some also fear they are losing self-control, freeze up, and miss many things that they could enjoy. They wait in vain for the giver to do "that something special." Unless the giver is a mind reader, they have no way to figure out what the passive receiver wants!

In actuality, you give when you receive. Most of us find pleasure in giving to our partner; and when they open themselves emotionally and physically to happily and actively receive from us, it is a gift that gives us additional pleasure.

Being an active receiver during sex is natural for some people, but unnatural and potentially difficult for others. If you are a passive receiver and want to become more active, you can learn a helpful technique to accomplish this by doing the CPR that follows below.

C P R:

To practice being an active receiver, take turns being a giver and a receiver. When it is your turn to receive, try going limp. Let all of your muscles relax. Take a deep breath to help start this process. If you feel like touching or giving, say so. Let your partner know and talk it through. We know that this will be difficult for some of you, but don't give in to the desire to give back. Be passive for ten full minutes. Stay focused on the sensations you are experiencing. If it is a positive experience for you, try making some sounds of pleasure or let the giver know what it feels like. Tell the giver if you would prefer a different pressure or touch, or if you would like focus on a certain area.

If you are the giver, you can help your partner by reminding them verbally, "this is about and for you." Remember that giving is not servicing your partner. Instead, it is a pleasurable gift to you both.

Write down three things you found enjoyable about being an active receiver and share them with your partner.

1. _____

2. _____

3. _____

Write down three things you enjoy about being giver and share them with your partner.

1. _____

2. _____

3. _____

REHEARSE

Learning new ways (or regaining old ways) of being romantic and sexual together does not come easily. Couples frequently struggle with "getting it right" and may give up if something fails to go as planned or hoped for, the efforts are seen as a total loss. The progress is no longer noted and the focus is on the problems rather then the solutions.

Professional ice skaters practice falling. They deliberately stumble so they can rehearse recovering, getting back on their feet, as quickly as possible. By rehearsing difficulties and giving yourself permission to have awkward moments during romantic or sexual activities, you and your partner can successfully navigate past them when they occur during actual lovemaking sessions.

C P R:

Discuss the possible difficulties that may arise, or that arose, while trying a CPR. Write some of them here:

| C |
| P |
| R |

_____

_____

_____

_____

_____

_____

Now agree to rehearse both the stumble and the recovery. For example, perhaps you agreed to try the striptease CPR. You predict that the one stripping will feel embarrassed, laugh, and that you will both wind up calling the whole thing off. Rehearse this scene, saying something like, "It's okay, dear, you can do it. Let's take a break and try again." Repeat this scenario several times. Once you feel you've got the hang of it, pick another CPR and try the same with it. You may want to try this with many different CPRs, as you will most likely find that it is fun and that it encourages communication and draws you both closer together.

RELAPSE

Perhaps you were on a good roll and made progress with this book, but a few things got in the way – one of you got too busy, lost interest, waited for the other to push ahead and it did not happen. Perhaps one of you even sabotaged the process. Now one or both of you is angry or hurt and you don't want to try any more.

Relapse is a natural occurrence in growth processes. Change is hard work and threatening. We sometimes feel like we're treading on thin ice, and that attempts to change often evoke frustration and disappointment. It is easy to have setbacks and disappoint our partner or ourselves. But that is not a valid reason to stop trying. If you settle at this point, you may find yourself in a worse state of mind than when you started this CPR program, due to a new sense of guilt and shame from failure.

C P R:

Assess where you actually are in the CPR program. Acknowledge the tools you have now that you did not have before. Build upon your progress rather than starting over again. It is very important to let go of blame and focus on what you have already achieved as a couple rather than on the setbacks and the long way you still have to go. Reassure each other. It helps ignite the willingness to keep working on the relationship.

List the new tools that you have gained from reading this CPR book so far:

_____

_____

_____

Jot down reassuring messages that you can give to your partner and yourself in order to be inspired to keep doing the CPR assignments:

_____

_____

_____

RELAX

It is difficult to let go and have carefree sex when we are tense, tired, or stressed. When we don't relax, we tend to internalize our stress, only to have it explode on those people closest to us – particularly, our partner. This can be severely damaging to the relationship and is an unproductive way to eliminate stress.

You probably know how important it is for you to relax after a hard day at work, before a big exam or when major life events occur. Relaxation is vital for all of us. It helps us let go of anxiety and prepares the body and mind for new challenges. If you have been at odds with each other, relaxing before starting a CPR experience can greatly help the potential outcome of your efforts.

C P R:

Relax together as a couple. Before starting any more CPRs, or revisiting them, agree to relax together for at least 10 minutes. Sit or lie down together in a spot that feels comfortable to both of you. Sit in silence together or play soft music. Do some breathing or stretching exercises together or do some cuddling or spoon breathing (see the previous "cuddle" CPR). Check in with each other to make sure you are both relaxed enough to move on to other CPRs, sex or other activities. Write how relaxing first changed the experience for you.

Now discuss your findings with your partner.

RELIGION

Many of us struggle with negative sexual attitudes and feelings of guilt and shame engendered by our religious upbringing and education. We are often afraid to touch ourselves, engage in oral or anal sex play, or to enjoy intercourse because of religious prohibitions and teachings. Besides this, there is often religious incompatibility, which occurs when religion is important to one partner and not to the other or when you don't share the same faith. Together, these issues can create serious relationship stress and sexual problems.

When religious issues cause problems in a couple's sex life, the situation is often made worse by the tendency of many couples to falsely believe that religion is too large an issue to handle, and that trying to resolve it is useless or impossible. The issues are then never addressed. It's time for a change. A positive attitude here may go a long way and help in finding solutions.

C P R:

C
P
R

Research your religious faith(s) together to find religious citations or messages about intimacy. You may be very surprised at what you learn. All religions contain at least some, if not many, positive messages about sex. They may be in the form of commandments to enjoy your loved one, psalms and songs that rejoice in the close sharing of love, and even actual instructions on how to have a happy and satisfying sex life. Share your findings together and see if you can incorporate some of them into your intimate times together.

If your religion is overly strict about sex or prohibits it except for purposes of conception, discuss these restrictions with your partner to reach a common understanding.

Most religions teach tolerance and acceptance toward others. Seek messages in your religion that show ways to love someone who does not ascribe to the same views that you have. Take time to learn about your partner's religious beliefs. See if you can respect your partner's differences in this area, and show that respect by making space for their religious expressions (or lack thereof). Communicate this acceptance to your partner. You may still have strong feelings about having religious differences, but you may find the differences to be much less of an obstacle to sex after you have taken the time to express yourselves.

If you have difficulty doing this CPR, consider speaking to a member, or members, of the clergy for enlightenment and guidance.

Positive messages about love and sex from our religions:

_____

_____

_____

REMEMBER

When times are tough in a relationship, some of us withdraw from our partner and wonder why we even choose to remain with them. By not remembering the positive aspects of our partner and our relationship, we focus only on the negative and that becomes our reality.

Remembering what initially attracted us to our partner and why we got together in the first place can be very helpful. Remembering how our courtship and sex life together was when it was at its best can also be useful. By revisiting these positive past experiences, many couples find a longing to experience them again and an enthusiasm to recreate some of the earlier, happier times. Besides, the act of remembering and reminiscing bonds partners by highlighting the best of the relationship.

C P R:

Start by remembering the anniversary of a special day in your relationship, such as your first date, first kiss, the day you moved in with each other, or your wedding date. Share your memories with each other. Look through old photos of the two of you, play "our song" and relive memories that way. Do this on a monthly basis. Yes! Monthly! Why wait for once a year when you can be remembering why you are together every month? And if time is an issue, take at least five minutes to acknowledge the special date on the calendar and share your thoughts, feelings and hopes about your relationship.

Next, answer the following questions and share what you've written with your partner. Use as much detail as you can so you may be able to recapture the feelings.

What attracted you to your partner?

_____

_____

What was your best date with your partner? Why?

_____

_____

What was your best sexual experience with your partner? Why?

_____

_____

RENDEVOUS

Rendezvous, the French expression for meeting, has taken on in English the meaning of a special date, one that connotes a sense of secrecy or personal connection outside of the norm. It implies two lovers getting together to express their passion for each other – something that is probably missing in your relationship, since you are reading this CPR book. Yet when you were courting, you probably went to great lengths to have secret, special getaways with your new partner. Now you have let life get in the way. Your time together mostly consist of meals, running errands together and sleeping. Where did those hot dates go?

C P R:

Rendezvous with your partner! Get away for romance! Get away for sex! If you can't find the time for an evening or weekend date, find a place and time where you can meet during the workday. Skip out for sex at lunchtime. Meet at the beach or park to make out on a blanket in the sand or on the grass. Or run home for a little bite to eat and some playtime. Keep this date a secret between you. And when you can schedule time away, plan a romantic vacation for just the two of you. Be sure to have a rendezvous at least once a month. Agree now on where you will go for your rendezvous this month and write it here:

C

P

R

_____

_____

_____

_____

RENEW VOWS

As you are working on resuscitating your sex life, there must have been a time when your attraction to each other was fresh, exciting and alive. At that point, most of you made vows to eternally love, respect and honor each other. Whether it was at a wedding, a civil union ceremony or during a toast of wine, when you decided to commit you most likely exchanged words that were deep in meaning to you both. By doing so, you demonstrated your love for each other and anticipated a loving future together.

Some of you may now feel that the vows made were not kept, and disillusionment has set in. Renewing your vows can help you recapture some of your former loving and happy feelings. It is also an opportunity to start afresh and create a new and happier relationship that is built from what you have learned from this book.

C P R:

Discuss the exact vows you made to each other. If you can't remember the actual words, at least discuss the intent you had at the time. Talk about your vows and pick ones you still find relevant. Add any new ones you feel are appropriate and write them all down. You may want to memorialize them formally – write them on pretty paper, print them out using a fancy font, carve them into wood or clay or paint them on a canvas.

Write the vows below:

_____

_____

_____

_____

_____

Read the vows to each other every month on the anniversary of the date when you exchanged either the old vows or the recent ones. Sharing the vows each month will keep them fresh in your minds and help inspire you to remember your deep love and commitment. You may even want to create a ceremony to officially renew vows, such as a second wedding or a commitment ceremony. Invite friends and family to witness the special day and help you celebrate!

RESPECT

We frequently hear our clients complain, "How can I be interested in sex with my partner when they don't show me respect?" It seems to be a no-brainer. Being respected by our partner increases our sexual desire. A lack of respect implies disapproval and is a major turn-off.

What is respect? Respect is very similar to love or passion. We all want it and we all think we know what it is. But there is no agreement as to what it actually means. It is very subjective. The words appreciation, awe, consideration, deference, honor, recognition, regard, reverence and value are all synonymous with respect. Mutual respect acts like a glue that mends relationship rifts and bonds a couple. It gets couples through the rough times. If you treat your partner with respect, it is highly likely that you will have both a wonderful relationship and a fulfilling sex life.

C P R:

First, find your own definition of respect. It's helpful to ask: "if my partner really respected me, then they would… or wouldn't…" Would what? Wouldn't what?

Jill's definition of respect: "He wouldn't call me names or put me down in public or in front of the kids. He wouldn't pressure me to do things I'm unwilling to do. He would trust me enough to share his innermost feelings with me."

Jack's definition of respect: "She would listen when I speak without interrupting me or contradicting me. She would show some recognition for my efforts at home and at work. She would be honest with me."

Now write your answer. If my partner respected me, they would… wouldn't…

_____

_____

Then ask yourself "how do I show my respect to my loved one?" Write down your answer.

_____

_____

_____

Next share these ideas with your partner. If you can find a mutual definition for respect, wonderful! Go with it. If you can't, that's okay. What's most important is that you both clearly understand how your partner defines it and what you need to be doing to meet their expectations of receiving respect from you. Finally, if you find your partner's specifications acceptable, then try to fulfill them. In other words, treat your partner with dignity and respect by showing what they believe to be demonstrations of respect.

RESPONSIBILITY

It's easy to see only our own side of a situation. This tunnel vision can lead us to a stalemate in our relationship, where we are constantly locking horns with our partners and blaming them for all that is wrong with our sex life. Perhaps you tell your partner that **they** are the problem; you label them sexually deficient; you tell them they will never change.

Barring disease or accident, a sex life rarely dwindles and dies due to one partner's behavior in a relationship. It takes two people to make it happen and two to make it end. Each of us is personally responsible for seeing to it that our sex life remains alive. Even if you feel that the problem is entirely your partner's fault, that you are always the one that works to keep the relationship alive, that you are tired of being the responsible one and that now it's your partner's turn, if you don't show effort and work with them on the CPRs, you will never make any progress.

Remember that it is the sexual relationship that is important here and not your accounting system of who did or didn't do something. If, for the moment, you have to make most of the effort to keep your sex life alive, then do it!

C P R:

Acknowledge that if you've been working with this book as a couple and have reached this point, you clearly have not done all the work yourself. Your partner is working with you and taking at least some responsibility. They must want what you want. Stubbornly holding on to your anger and frustration is now the major obstacle blocking you from reaching your goals. Find a way to release your resentment – for example, strenuous exercise, yoga or verbally venting to a friend. Give in and do more. Agree to be equal partners during each CPR exercise.

RITUAL

We all have rituals that help us avoid, or invite, having sex. Avoiding rituals include such things as working late into the night, falling asleep watching TV, working on the computer way past your partner's bedtime, stuffing yourself with food (making you bloated and uncomfortable), or going to bed with a face full of cream. These rituals interfere with closeness, are damaging and taint the sexual encounter.

Inviting rituals can enhance sexuality, making the sexual activity feel more meaningful, and in some cases, more sacred. Carlos and Olga found that bathing together before bedtime was a positive ritual while other clients enjoyed reading aloud to each other. Some couples find that lighting candles together or offering special blessings to each other can lead them to feeling more appreciated and desired. It also gives them a sense of joint purpose and helps solidify a sense of coming together.

C P R:

Create your own inviting ritual together. Discuss what might make a sexual encounter more sacred, more meaningful for you both. You can incorporate something from your spiritual practices or even something that is light and fun. Prior to sex, light candles, practice breathing together, gaze in each other's eyes, give your partner a sensual massage or footbath, or bathe together. Share a glass of wine or fruit juice, play a sexual board game or read a romantic poem to each other.

List some rituals that you would like to introduce into your relationship.

C

P

R

1. _____

2. _____

3. _____

ROLE PLAY

When we tell our clients to do a specific sexual assignment, some of them say, "I can't. It's not natural. It's just not me." They are afraid to move beyond their comfort level and take the risks necessary to create a satisfying sex life. If this applies to you, what we have found works in these cases is for you to pretend to be an actor playing a role. Most actors are shy people, yet on the stage or screen they appear fearless and outgoing. Acting like someone else allows you to shed inhibitions and take full advantage of the CPRs.

C P R:

Pick a sexual activity you would like to become comfortable with but fear trying. It might be something your partner has asked for on their Conditions for Good Sex list, something you have seen in a movie, read about in a book or simply know of and want to try. Think of how you would act if you were comfortable with this activity. Note the way you think you would look and move and what you would wear and say. For example, if you were learning how to have an orgasm, you might thrash around, arch and stiffen your body, breathe heavily, moan and scream.

Write down a sexual activity that you want to try.

_____

_____

_____

Write down what kind of role playing you need to do to make this activity more comfortable for you.

_____

_____

_____

Try your chosen sexual activity as many times as is necessary for you to find the comfort level with it that you seek.

ROMANCE

Americans value and thrive on romance. Little children learn through fairytales that the romantic ideal has Prince Charming riding up on his white horse, sweeping the fair maiden off her feet and carrying her off into the sunset to live "happily ever after."

As teens and adults we are bombarded with media messages about romance. Advertisements, movies, TV, pop songs and novels send strong signals that romance is vital if you want to live the American Dream. In fact, we have a national holiday called Valentine's Day that is dedicated to nothing but romance! The adventurous, mysterious aura of romance gets our adrenaline pumping. It's no wonder that romance has been referred to as a drug; the more we get, the more we want!

Of course, after you've been together with your partner for years, the wild romantic gestures of courtship generally get replaced with quieter, less dramatic but very important demonstrations of love and romance based on small day-to-day kindnesses to each other. Yet when romance is totally absent, sexual relationships can become platonic, boring or even nonexistent.

Giving flowers, chocolates, perfume, jewelry, poetry and uttering sweet words are but a few of the multitude ways by which we demonstrate romantic intent. Some other ways include things like helping your partner with chores or listening to them or holding them when they are troubled or down. Look at your checklist from the beginning of this book. Many of the conditions you listed for good sex are your own personal definitions of romance.

To be truly romantic, however, you must achieve the right state of mind before engaging in acts of romance. If you are just doing romantic things to please your partner, but don't feel it in your heart, your partner will sense that — and these activities won't work.

C P R:

Try making today, or each day, Valentine's Day for your partner. What you do doesn't have to be expensive or dramatic, like hiring a plane to fly over your home and skywrite your partner's name, or whisking them off to Paris (although you could certainly do those things if you can afford them!). Simple, inexpensive gestures can be very effective, as long as you do things for your partner that you know they would consider to be romantic: surprise them with a picnic dinner at dusk, serenade them outside the bedroom window, send them an I Love You card or note every day of the year. If you have trouble coming up with your own romantic ideas, buy a book on romance and mark the ideas you especially like. If your partner does the same, you will have quite a list!

Romantic behaviors that would be meaningful to me:

1. _____

2. _____

3. _____

ROSE-COLORED GLASSES

During courtship we tend to see our partners through rose-colored glasses. We only see the positive part of their character and ignore their faults. We think they are perfect and fall in love with this idealized version. As time goes by, however, the rosy hue of romantic love begins to fade. Our partner's imperfections and faults emerge and consume us, and the lenses of our glasses change from rose-colored to gray.

We may let these feelings stew inside, or express them to our partner; but either way, we harm the relationship. We also hurt ourselves by viewing our partner in a negative light, because we begin to feel that something is wrong with us for remaining in a relationship with such a "flawed" person.

C P R:

Put the rose-colored glasses back on! Focus on your partner's virtues or special attributes. Make a list of at least three special things that you see in your partner:

1. _____

2. _____

3. _____

Carry this list with you and review it each day as a constant reminder of your partner's good points and why you love them.

C

P

R

ROYAL TREATMENT

You have probably thought at some point, "Oh, if only I were a king/queen, I'd…" Most of us have these kinds of fantasies but of course few of us will ever have the chance to actually sit on a throne. We can however, with the cooperation of our partner, be queen or king for a day. Yet few of us make the time and effort to treat our loved one with the respect and pampering that royalty receives. We focus too much on our own issues and needs, assuming our partner knows that we love them. Giving our partner royal treatment shows them how important and special they are to us. Our clients frequently report a belief that they would be much more sexually interested in their partner if their partner treated them like they were very special.

C P R:

Treat your partner like royalty for one day. Pick a day that will work for you both. Wake up before your partner, make yourself presentable and prepare yourself to be there for them, just as anyone serving royalty might do. Then take care of them and nurture them. Serve them breakfast in bed. Give them a massage. Take them for a relaxing, scenic drive. Take care of the kids.

Give your partner a day for themselves. Note that this may mean doing the chores that your partner normally does. Design a day that makes them feel special and use whatever means necessary, even if it means arranging a getaway or a babysitter for the kids. Be sure to use terms of endearment toward them and let them know that you love them. Repeat this type of day at least every three months.

Write three things that you will do to give your partner royal treatment:

1. _____

2. _____

3. _____

Look at your calendar and choose and set aside a day now for your first attempt at giving your partner royal treatment.

_____

RUTS

Sexual patterns are developed early in a relationship and couples tend to stick with these patterns with little, if any, deviation. We fall into a rut and are leery of trying new things or of suggesting change. Perhaps we are afraid of hurting our partner's feelings, or of being seen as abnormal – or even of raising suspicion of an affair if we come up with a novel suggestion. We don't want to ruin what "appears" to work, so we end up immobilized and stuck in a rut. Sex becomes routine, predictable and boring, and then often avoided altogether.

C P R:

Agree to take some risks, within mutually acceptable boundaries, to add some novelty to your sex life. Then surprise your partner with, for example, a new sex toy, a new touch, a new position or a new location. Share a fantasy, watch an erotic video, or buy a book on sexual positions and try something new you see in it. And of course do the CPR suggestions in this book!

List three new activities you will try:

1. _____

2. _____

3. _____

C

P

R

NOTES:

_____

_____

_____

_____

_____

_____

_____

_____

_____

_____

CHAPTER 5

Advanced CPR's

CLIMAX I & II (SIMULTANEOUS ORGASM)

CLITORIS (AND OTHER GENITALIA) COITUS

COMPENSATE (PHYSICAL, DESIRE & ERECTION PROBLEMS)

CONTRACEPTION CUNNILINGUS & FELLATIO (ORAL SEX)

PENIS, PERINEUM & MORE PLAYING DOCTOR I & II PLAYTHINGS

POSITIONS PENETRATION VS. CONTAINMENT PORNOGRAPHY

RAPID (PREMATURE) EJACULATION RESTRAINING REVISIT REVIEW

PLAYING DOCTOR –
BY YOURSELF

We can't be totally free sexually if our genital anatomy is a mystery to us. We can't fully use and enjoy parts of our body if we know little about them. And yet most American women have never seen their genitals since they are hidden away between the legs, out of normal range of view! Many are embarrassed to take a mirror and look to see what's really down there. While many heterosexual men have looked at both their female partner's genitals and the genitals of females in pornography, few have looked close enough to totally discern the genital structure. For example, it is still a common misconception that women only have two holes: one for defecating (the anus) and one for sexual intercourse, delivering a baby and urinating (the vagina). Many miss the urethra, which is solely for urination, even when looking right at it. Similarly, while men's genitals can easily be seen, few men or women have ever seen the man's anus and perineum, or viewed the testicles from behind. Examining the genitals can be highly educational – and fun at the same time.

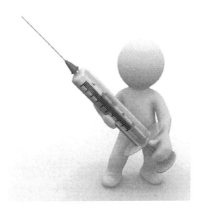

C P R:

For the Woman:

Chart your vulva (the external female genitalia). Take a hand mirror and examine your genitals. Find your mons (the hairy area above the clitoris), your outer lips, your inner lips, your clitoris, and your urethral and vaginal openings. Do a thorough examination. See where everything is located and how it looks. If you are unfamiliar with the female genital structure, refer to the diagram below.

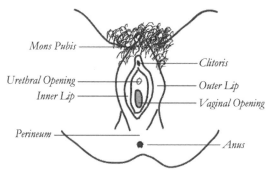

For the Man:

You are no doubt more familiar with your genitals than the average woman is with hers, since the male genitals are external. But if you have never seen the back of your scrotum and testicles, your perineum and your anal opening, examine these areas in a hand mirror and become familiar with them.

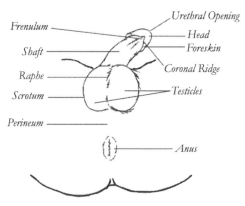

PLAYING DOCTOR II –
FOR THE COUPLE

As children, we had a natural curiosity to explore our bodies and those of others. Playing doctor, a favorite childhood game for most of us, was, in many cases a lead-up to "you show me yours and I'll show you mine." It allowed us to see and investigate other kids' genitals. As we aged, however, some of us learned to attach a certain level of shame with regard to our genitals- even in the presence of a partner who we loved and who we knew loved us. The percentage of couples who engage in sexual activities in the dark and never look at each other's bodies is large. If you and your partner fall into this category, here is your chance to change things. If you both are comfortable and "out there" with your bodies, then make this exercise a refresher course.

C P R:

Well, it's time to play doctor again! Make this CPR fun. This is mainly an exploratory exercise. The genitals will be examined and touched but there will be no sexual stimulation of them. Take turns with the two roles in this CPR exercise. One of you will be the doctor and the other the patient. When done, switch roles.

Start with the basics, such as checking the eyes, the ears and the heart. Then examine the genitals. Chart and explore the genitals in detail. You and your partner may have been together for many years and yet never closely examined each other. One or both of you may be embarrassed or feel vulnerable or uncomfortable doing a genital examination or being examined genitally, but it will be well worth the effort if you follow through. You will in all probability become a better lover.

Gently, and with loving consideration of your partner's vulnerability, examine and name the parts. Pay attention to the shape, texture and color of the genitals and the pubic hair.

If you find it too stressful to do this CPR for any length of time, do a start and stop technique where you stop the activity when your emotions get too intense, cover up and then talk to your partner or cuddle. Resume the exercise as soon as you feel comfortable. Stop and start as many times as you need to complete this assignment.

Referring to the diagram, in the man, look for and point to or touch:

- *the shaft of the penis and the foreskin, if any;*

- *the head (glans) of the penis with its urethral opening on top;*

- *the coronal ridge – the very sensitive rim on the underside of the head of the penis;*

- *the frenulum – a tiny, sensitive spot found at 12 o'clock on the underside of the glans;*

- *the scrotal sac with the testicles inside;*

- *the raphe (the line down the middle of the scrotal sac);*

- *the perineum (the smooth skin between the scrotal sac and the anal opening);*

- *the anal opening.*

Referring to the diagram, in the woman, look for:

- *the mons (the hairy mound);*

- *the outer lips (hair covered flaps continuing down from the mons). The hair on both the mons and outer lips(also known as labia) thins out after menopause;*

- *the inner lips (inner labia). Gently spread apart the outer lips to examine the inner lips. See if the inner lips are "innies" (thin and close to the body) or "outies" (fleshy, protruding and configured in various shapes). See if both lips are the same shape or different shapes (very common) and whether they are the same shade or different shades (also common). Are there skin tags? Veins?*

- *the clitoris. Is it lightly hooded or heavily hooded or double hooded? Gently pull the hood up to see the clitoris. Does it look like a single pearl-like structure or does it look like there are two pearls (a bifurcated clitoris)?*

- *Look closely for the urethral opening. It is NOT inside the vagina, but somewhere on the vulva above the vaginal opening.*

- *Finally, find the vaginal and anal openings.*

Jot down three new or interesting things that you found from examining your own body:

1._____

2._____

3._____

Jot down three things that you learned from examining your partner's body:

C

P

R

1._____

2._____

3._____

CLITORIS (AND OTHER GENITALIA)

A great many women, and even more men, are unfamiliar with how the female genital anatomy looks and how to best pleasure and arouse it. The appearance of each woman's genitalia (vulva) is unique. It varies in shape, size, color, placement of labia and urethra.

Contrary to what many people think, it is the clitoris and not the vagina that is the woman's chief sex organ. The clitoris is the only body part whose sole function is to experience erotic pleasure. It is equivalent in structure to an uncircumcised penis in that it has a shaft, a head and a hood, and gets hard when sexually stimulated. And just like the head of the penis, the clitoris is packed with nerve endings and thus is very sensitive, while only the outer third of the vagina is capable of feeling sexual pleasure! The inner two-thirds of the vaginal walls have few nerve endings and feel mainly pressure. Among the women who experience orgasms, approximately two-thirds of them do not "come" solely from the penis thrusting in the vagina. They need clitoral contact or stimulation.

The more familiar you both are with the clitoris and how to stimulate it, the more likely it is that passion will be restored in your relationship, and that sex will be something to look forward to.

C P R:

C

P

R

For the Woman:

In the previous "playing doctor" CPR, you looked at your vulva and identified its parts. Now that you are familiar with how your genitals look, it is time to learn what types of touching each part likes. There are no rules and no correct way to touch your genitals. It takes experimentation to discover what works for you.

Start by stoking your entire vulva. Perhaps you prefer a very light, almost tickling type of stroke; or you may prefer a deep, kneading, massaging type stroke, or a combination of the two. Next, stroke your clitoris. See if you like to be touched directly on the head of the clitoris, to the left or right of it, or above it. Do you like a firm stroke or a light stroke? Do you prefer touching yourself with a dry hand or a lubricated hand?

Now insert a finger or fingers into the outer third of the vagina and go "around the clock," stroking the walls of the vagina while moving in a clockwise direction. See where, if at all, there is pleasurable sensation.

This may be an uncomfortable assignment for some of you if you have never looked at or touched yourself, but it can be most enlightening and empowering to be familiar and comfortable with your body.

For the Couple:

You have already found the various parts of the vulva together during the "playing doctor" CPR. Now explore together how your partner best likes these parts to be touched and stimulated, while getting constant feedback from the partner being touched.

Stroke the entire vulva first. Try different kinds of strokes, and even tug gently on the labia (inner and outer lips). Try touching the clitoris in ways you've never done before. Pretend that there is a tiny bubble between the clitoris and your finger and that your task is to gently rub the bubble around on the tip of the clitoris without breaking it. Try the clitoral touching with both dry fingers and lubricated fingers.

Something to remember when you are stimulating your partner's clitoris for arousal is that **the clitoris plays hide and seek**. When a woman first gets sexually excited, the clitoris gets firm, just like a penis does when aroused. When a woman is close to orgasm, however, the clitoris often retracts and seems to disappear. Many people are confused by this behavior, thinking that the woman is no longer "turned on", while in fact the opposite is actually true. If you continue stimulating the area, the clitoris will still be stimulated. It's not gone; it's just hiding under cover.

When you have completed the clitoral touching, slide you fingers down to the vaginal opening. Women frequently enjoy the "around the clock" check of the vagina, in which a lubricated finger is inserted into the vagina and then systematically moved to different positions that match the numbers on a clock. Certain numbers, when stimulated, will feel more pleasurable than others to your partner.

Also try finding the Grafenberg spot ("G-spot"), a sensitive area just behind the front wall of the vagina. When orgasm occurs from stimulation of this spot, some women experience a gush of fluid known as "female ejaculate". As with the male, the fluid is distinctly different from urine and usually only occurs in response to intense sexual pleasure. Look for the G-spot by inserting a finger into the vagina, bending the tip back up behind the pubic bone, and exploring the area of the vagina that is a bit rough and ridged (as opposed to the rest of the vagina which is smooth). Different finger motions will feel better to different women, and may even vary in pleasure for the same woman on different occasions. Many report that the "windshield wiper" motion, in which the inserted finger is rubbed from side to side (much like a windshield wiper on a car), with a bit of a curving down on each side, is more effective than an in and out motion.

In addition, remember not to grab or grope at the genitals or the breasts. Most women do not like this until they are aroused, and most often not even then. And don't forget to get constant feedback from your partner while you are touching her so that you learn to touch her in the ways that are most pleasing and arousing to her. If you learn the kind of stroke your partner likes, both on the genitals and the remainder of the body, and pleasure her in that way, your sex life should take a most positive turn.

Take lots of time and make this assignment a prolonged sensuous adventure and learning experience. Do this CPR even if you are a lesbian couple. Everyone's body is different, so don't assume that because you know how your own body works, that your partner's body will react the same way.

Jot down three things you found new or interesting about touching your partner's genitals:

1._____

2._____

3._____

For the woman: What did you learn from viewing and touching your genitals?

1._____

2._____

3._____

C

P

R

PENIS, PERINEUM & MORE

Did you know that the penis reacts to thoughts and emotions? It most certainly does!

A penis will not positively respond to stimulation if the mind is disturbed with fears or negative thoughts. At those times, even if a man is in bed with a sexy and willing partner, he can't will an erection, no matter how aroused he is mentally.

And while the penis is usually tough, it can be hurt if a touch is too strong, involves too much twisting or too much friction. Most men don't complain when their penis is touched incorrectly. They typically bear it, thinking that complaining may result in their partner shying away from touching them altogether. Men are also reluctant to ask that you touch either their perineum or their anal opening. They may not realize how good it can feel to have these area touched or are embarrassed to ask. In both cases, sexual desire and pleasure are not being realized.

C P R:

The penis does not stop once it reaches the torso. It continues on, inside the body just below the skin, to the edge of the anus. This smooth area, between the base of the penis and the anus, is called the perineum and is an area of potentially great physical pleasure. The same is true for the frenulum, the rim on the underside of the head of the penis. To heighten desire and pleasure, try touching your partner's penis and perineum with no other goal than to discover what feels good and what does not. This will require verbal communication and cooperation. If you are the man who is being touched, be sure to give honest feedback to your partner as they explore these parts of your body.

Begin by stoking the shaft of the penis, experimenting with the firmness and speed of your strokes. Run your hand up to the head of the penis, encircle the head inside your hand as if making a fist, and roll the head. Take your fingers and run them around the rim of the head and try to find the frenulum, an exquisitely sensitive spot at 12 o'clock on the underside of the rim. Remember to get feedback from your partner all along. This is especially important when it comes to the perineum, as partners may not be familiar with this as an erogenous zone (i.e., one that produces sexual pleasure). Try stroking it, tapping it gently Do these exercises with a dry hand and a lubricated hand and see which method is more arousing for your partner.

Next, explore the scrotum and the raphe (the line down the middle of the scrotal sac). Carefully squeeze the testicles, cup the entire scrotum and tug down just a bit. Many men also like being touched at the anal opening. If you are both interested, try inserting a lubricated finger (making sure the nail is properly trimmed as to cause no harm) into the anus and up to the prostate gland. Men frequently describe a gentle prostate massage as the utmost of sexual pleasures.

If you have never touched these parts of a man's body before, you may find exploring them to be quite interesting, and perhaps, exciting.

Do this exercise with your partner even if you are a gay couple. Gay men usually think they know what their partner will like because they know what they themselves like and the equipment is the same. But while you may have the same parts, everyone is different; so make sure you don't skip this CPR.

COITUS II

By now, you have completed a good part of this book, and hopefully, have achieved a level of intimacy that was previously missing in your relationship. If you have adhered to the ban on coitus, this would be a good time to re-introduce it, along with other sexual activities, provided you both feel ready and feel that you've worked out those issues that kept you from looking forward to sex.

As you've progressed through this CPR book, most of you have likely picked up new tools that will enhance your sexual interactions. Don't abandon them now that the ban on coitus has been lifted. These are tools for you to use for the remainder of your life! If you let these tools rust from lack of use, you will revert to your dead, dying, dull or dissatisfying sex life.

C P R:

Don't leap right into intercourse. Follow the pattern that we've laid out for you. Start with charting the genitals, kissing, caressing and petting, and over the course of days or weeks, work your way up to penetration and thrusting. Add condiments to the mix and vary them so that you don't fall back into a rut. Also, remember that communication with your partner is vital.

By now you have learned what your conditions for good sex are and what pleases you.

If your conditions are not being met, be sure to let your partner know what element is missing for you so that you can both enjoy loving and satisfying sex.

C

P

R

CLIMAX

Climax is another word for orgasm or "coming." If you have never had a climax, it's hard to describe the physiological sensation. Orgasm is an explosive release of neuromuscular tension at the height of sexual arousal. This is usually accompanied by ejaculation of sperm and semen in the male and vaginal contractions in the female.

Some interesting differences exist between men and women when it comes to climaxing and having orgasms. For example, the average adult male has had thousands of ejaculations in his life and yet may never have had an orgasm. It is a common misconception that ejaculation and orgasm are the same, but in males, an ejaculation is a bodily function that can occur with or without orgasm. In fact, it is not uncommon for men to ejaculate when they have their first digital prostate exam (when the doctor inserts a finger into the man's anus and touches the prostate to assess it's size and firmness), a procedure few men find sexually arousing, and certainly not one they would describe as orgasmic.

At the same time, men may also learn how to have incredible orgasms without ejaculation. This is partially due to the fact that an orgasm is not only the spasms that occur in and around the genitals, but may also be the incredible emotional experience that often occurs coincidently with the spasms that most people think are an orgasm. We find substantial evidence for this difference in both our work with people with disabilities who can no longer feel their genitals, but are able to have fantastic orgasms just the same. And in Tantra (traditionally defined as "weaving" and "sacred sexual practices"), orgasms for men are frequently described as better, stronger, and more intense, when they do not include a simultaneous ejaculation). Further evidence is found in men who ejaculate during sexual activities while high on methamphetamines. They report no pleasure and, in many cases, experience pain.

Another way that men and women differ is that men frequently will ejaculate when they reach the point of ejaculatory inevitability – the point where they are aware of being about to ejaculate – (again, falsely labeling this orgasm), even if stimulation is stopped. While there are methods on how to deal with ejaculation control, most men chose not to learn them. They ejaculate when they reach this point because they feel they must. A woman, on the other hand, can get right to the point of orgasm and still not "come" if stimulation is stopped or there is an outside interference. For example, if a child were to knock on the bedroom door just when a woman feels that she is on the verge of orgasm, the orgasm might no longer occur and arousal would decline quickly. Many women are also able to ejaculate. Unlike the man, however, it is almost always coinciding with an orgasm.

Many people, but especially women, find that they can fully enjoy sex without climaxing. They take pleasure from the physical and emotional closeness that generally accompanies sex. However, their partners, both male and female, so much want them to have an orgasm that some women fake them. A 2005 British study claims that 92% of the women they interviewed reported having faked orgasm at least once in order to protect their partner's ego. While climaxing is not necessary for enjoying sex, if you've never experienced it, you may indeed find sex boring. Furthermore, if a climax isn't achieved, you may wrongly assume that sex wasn't good.

For the Woman:

There are several common reasons why women might fail to have a climax. The first has to do with difficulties such as unresolved anger or power issues in the relationship. In this case, the woman has had orgasms in the past, or currently has them when she is by herself, but is not able to have them with her partner. Lack of orgasm can also be a side effect of prescription drugs; exhaustion; lack of, or limited, foreplay or lack of clitoral stimulation.

In other cases, some women know what it would take for them to be orgasmic with their partner but have difficulty in communicating this, while others have not learned how to reach orgasm, much less tell their partners how to help them in this regard.

For the Man:

There are several common reasons why men may fail to climax. The first one is the same as for women. There is an emotional piece to the relationship that is inhibiting the orgasm. For men, this typically involves some sort of power struggle with his partner that is being played out in the sexual arena. For example, the woman might not be letting the man have a say in sex.

The second common reason men may not reach an orgasm has to do with the lack of understanding what an orgasm is, falsely believing the ejaculation is an orgasm, as described above.

A third reason has to do with drug use: both prescription (such as antidepressants) and illicit (such as methamphetamines and cocaine). Drugs of this sort commonly cause a lack of interest in sex, difficulty in achieving an erection and problems ejaculating. Consult with your doctor to see if there are other prescription medications available that have fewer negative sexual side effects. Jack's doctor lowered the dosage of Jack's antidepressant medication and Jack found, that in a short while, he was able to feel desire and achieve erections again.

Recreational drugs are commonly more difficult to deal with as we have widespread "acceptance" of such drugs in our culture. Adding to the problem is that the negative side-effects evolve slowly with continued drug use and by then, most people are addicted. It is obviously essential for good physical and mental health and a satisfying sex life, to stop using illicit drugs. While this is easier said than done, we strongly urge anyone caught in the self- destructive pattern of drug use to get help. Check local treatment programs or call a national hotline such as Narcotics Anonymous.

C P R:

For the Woman:

There are several highly successful self-help books and videos on the market dealing with this topic. They all boil down to the same basic steps, which include the following:

- *Conduct a self-sex history: review the details of your sex life from its beginning to today.*
- *Deal with unresolved issues that may become apparent from the sex history.*
- *Explore your body.*
- *Explore self-pleasuring of the entire body.*
- *Explore genital self-stimulation.*
- *Role-play movements and noises that are associated with climaxing.*
- *Teach your partner what you've learned.*

For the Man:

As with the women, for men there are several highly successful self-help books and videos on the market dealing with this topic. They include the following basis steps:

- *Conduct a self-sex history: review the details of your sex life from its beginning to today.*
- *Deal with unresolved issues that may become apparent from the sex history.*
- *Deal with any unresolved issues in the relationship.*
- *Explore self-pleasuring and sensation awareness of the entire body.*
- *Explore genital self-stimulation utilizing new positions, methods and fantasies.*
- *Look into the partners eyes during sex.*
- *Learn to move the sexual energy up from the genitals into the heart.*
- *Learn ejaculation control.*
- *Role-play movements and noises that are associated with climaxing.*
- *Teach your partner what you've learned.*

CLIMAX II – SIMULTANEOUS ORGASM

Simultaneous orgasm, where both partners experience their climax at the same time, is considered the ideal by many couples. They claim that intercourse is just not as good as it could be without it. And certainly, if both partners prefer climaxing at the same time, then they should continue sex as usual. But for most of us, the push for simultaneous orgasms sets goals and imposes expectations on us, creating performance anxiety. Not only are we supposed to climax during sex, but we are also supposed to do it at the exact moment that our partner does! Furthermore, if one partner in a relationship has the belief that simultaneous orgasm is the "right" way to orgasm and the other does not, bad feelings and arguments often ensue.

The expectation of simultaneous orgasm interferes with both our capacity to devote our complete attention to sexually gratifying our partner, and with fully experiencing our own sexual pleasure. Instead of being able to relax, focus on, and enjoy the sexual buildup in our body, we have to shift concentration and focus on our partner's arousal level as well. Then we either hold back our climax or speed it up, depending on our perceptions of our partner's "readiness."

This so-called ideal is not only imposed on orgasms that occur during intercourse but also those that occur during the "sixty-nine" position of oral sex, where one partner lies upside down, or sideways, over the body of their partner so that each partner's mouth is positioned against the genitals of the other, with each orally stimulating their partner. This, just like striving for simultaneous orgasms, is another example of doing two things at once, which for most of us is extremely distracting.

C P R:

Take turns assisting each other to orgasm – either manually, orally, mechanically (with a vibrator) or during penetration. As the giver, take joy from your partner's pleasure as you watch their arousal buildup and the ensuing release. Even if your partner does not experience climax, help them get to the greatest height of pleasure that they can reach. This method puts full focus on the pleasure that each of you is experiencing, without having to worry about timing your orgasm. Even if you and your partner regularly experience and enjoy simultaneous orgasms, do this CPR.

C

P

R

CUNNILINGUS & FELLATIO (ORAL SEX)

Cunnilingus and fellatio are more commonly referred to as oral sex – that is, the use of the mouth, lips, tongue or teeth to stimulate the genitalia. Cunnilingus (also called "going down" or "eating") is oral sex performed on a woman. Fellatio (also called a "blow job" or "giving head") is oral sex performed on a man.

Some people find the thought of oral sex dirty and repugnant since we urinate through the genitals, and in the case of women, secrete and menstruate from the vagina. Unlike the vagina, the penis is predominantly external and so is much easier to clean. That's why fellatio is performed more than cunnilingus. Many men who insist that their partners give them a "blow job" would not dream of "going down" on their female partners in return. This is a source of resentment in many women and causes friction in sexual relationships.

Even when a woman gladly performs fellatio on a man, friction often arises concerning the swallowing of ejaculate. Some men believe that their partner does not love them if they won't swallow the semen. This is seldom true. To swallow or not to swallow is usually based on a woman's prior sex education, messages and experiences. Interestingly, many of the men who demand that their partner swallow the semen have never tasted or swallowed their own semen (or anybody else's).

Oral sex can produce intensely pleasurable sexual sensations for both sexes. If you haven't tried it because it makes you uncomfortable, check out the anxiety ladder in the P chapter, under "phobias." See if you can overcome or diminish your discomfort. If you can't, or the whole idea of oral sex turns you off, it doesn't mean that you are sexually incompetent. There are many other sexual activities that you can enjoy.

If, however, not engaging in oral sex is a bone of contention in your relationship and causes repeated arguments and sexual distancing, you may want to try some of the CPR techniques listed below. You might even learn to enjoy it!

C P R:

C
P
R

For Cunnilingus:

Shower or bathe together, giving extra attention to cleansing the genital area so that you are sure that you have eliminated any scent that offends you.

When you perform oral sex, if you need to add a barrier between your mouth and the female genitalia to make it more comfortable for you, cover the area with things such as chocolate syrup, whipped cream, wine or other beverage and then lick it off.

As for the actual act of cunnilingus, there is not one specific way to perform it. You can lick, kiss, or suck the clitoris, labia and vagina in any manner that pleases your partner. If you are enjoying it or getting aroused by doing cunnilingus, let your partner know, as many women worry that their partners get bored or even disgusted doing this.

For Fellatio:

Once again, remember that there is no one way to orally pleasure a partner.

If performing fellatio concerns you because you are afraid that you will gag on the penis, then kiss and lick and suck the outside of the penis from top to bottom (as if you were playing a harmonica) without taking it in your mouth. If you decide to take the penis in your mouth, a way to begin is by putting the soft penis in your mouth. The penis is smaller then than when erect, so you can get used to the sensation without gagging. You also don't have to take the entire penis in your mouth. You can just suck on the head of the penis and use your hand to stimulate the rest. You may also want to suck on or lick the scrotum and testicles.

If you are worried about the man ejaculating in your mouth or swallowing the ejaculate, you can stop the penile stimulation prior to ejaculation, or pull away as soon as ejaculation has begun. If you can't pull away in time, rather than swallowing the semen, you have the option of spitting out the semen or transferring it to your partner's mouth. Some women love the intimacy of having a man ejaculate in their mouth, and others don't. Stay within your comfort limits.

If your mouth or jaw gets tired because your partner needs extensive oral stimulation, alternate between using your mouth and using your hand to stimulate the genitals. If oral sex doesn't excite you, don't worry about it, but remember that it can be a thrilling and very intimate form of lovemaking.

POSITIONS

Many couples start their sex life together by exploring different sexual positions. They then settle into a routine, using just a few of them. Others never explore; they engage in only one or two positions, not realizing there are an endless amount of variations.

Trying new positions can not only spice up things, it can also relieve problems you may be having with sexual contact that might have arisen from things such as age, an accident or disease. If you feel any anxiety at the thought of venturing into new territory by trying out new positions, remember that for heterosexual couples there are really only six basic positions – man on top, woman on top, sideways entry, entry from behind, sitting or standing. Every variation beyond that is based on the positioning of the body and legs.

C P R:

C

P

R

Buy an illustrated book on sexual positions such as the Kama Sutra or any of the Anne Hooper books. Or, if you already have one, revisit it.

It's helpful to look through a book on positions at non-sexual times and discuss with each other what positions might interest you. You can then refer to the book as a visual guide when you are sexual with each other. Some positions might seem awkward at first and may even evoke laughter, but if they appeal to you on the page, try them several times before giving up and moving on.

Write down three sexual positions you and your partner have not tried and are willing to when the time is right.

1._____

2._____

3._____

REVISIT

As you went through this book, you might remember that we suggested that you go slowly and first build emotional closeness and intimacy before you worked on building sexual intimacy. Therefore, you were told in certain CPRs to revisit them once you reached the final chapter of this book, where coitus and overt sexual behavior were reintroduced to your relationship.

C P R:

The areas to revisit now are:

• *COMPROMISE – You were making compromises about where to vacation and what color to paint a room. Now make compromises regarding sexual timing, frequency, behaviors or whatever other compromises are needed in your relationship.*

• *CUDDLE – Instead of just holding each other when clothed, refer to the spooning exercise where you cuddle against each other's naked bodies.*

• *PERFORMANCE ANXIETY – You practiced doing "mind talk" while being touched. Now practice it during sexual stimulation and intercourse.*

• *PROLONG – Instead of only prolonging touch and kissing, now add prolonging intercourse. Slow down the strokes and prolong the enjoyment, arousal and intimacy.*

C

P

R

PLAYTHINGS (SEX TOYS)

Playthings are designed to enhance sexual pleasure. They can bring great fun and satisfaction to your sex life. Some people, however, struggle with various misconceptions about these sex toys that keep them from playing with them. Some falsely believe that they shouldn't need these toys to make sex more enjoyable, and that using toys to enhance sex means they are not skilled lovers. Others erroneously believe that if a woman enjoys these kinds of toys then she will grow to prefer the toy over the person and reject her partner altogether; or that men who enjoy such toys are homosexual or unmanly. Certain people feel that sex toys are unnatural and even evil. For some, the problem lies in not knowing a safe and comfortable way of purchasing sex toys.

Playthings can help enhance pleasure by reaching parts of the body, such as the G-spot, that are otherwise difficult or impossible to reach by hand or mouth. Many add an enjoyable vibrating motion and an intensity of sensation that just can't be produced in any other way. The added sensations of pleasure can help bring couples closer together.

Women typically respect and appreciate a partner's willingness to use sex toys. The playthings are seen as extensions of their partner, not a replacement. Clients commonly report that the use of sex toys adds to the mutual joy of sex between them and their partners. One who can skillfully use a sex toy is usually seen as an excellent lover.

C P R:

Examine your own view of sex toys. Ask yourself the following questions and jot down some thoughts on each:

Am I comfortable with adding playthings to our sex life?

_____

What is keeping me from being comfortable if I am not already so?

_____

What do I need to do to become comfortable with playthings?

_____

What playthings would I like to try with my partner?

_____

Now share these thoughts with each other. If you both agree to try some playthings, one option is to go to an adult store, if there is one close enough to your home. On the other hand, many people prefer the comfort, convenience and privacy of shopping at home instead. Look together at a few of the online adult toy company websites, such as Good Vibrations, Libida.com, Adam and Eve or the Sinclair Institute. Pick out a few items you both agree to try and order them.

When your playthings arrive, examine and discuss them before your next sex encounter date. See how they feel, talk about what you may or may not want to do with them. When you try them out, have fun. Remember, it's an experiment to see if you enjoy them. Keep the toys you enjoy handy for future encounters.

Also, be sure to agree, in advance, that each of you is free to state, without argument, that a particular toy is not to your liking. Set this toy aside. You may decide to try it again in the future. It usually takes three tries to really decide if we like a sexual activity or not. So be patient.

RESTRAINING

Many couples are intrigued by the concept of bondage and domination (also known as BDSM), yet are afraid to try this form of sex play. This is usually due to a lack of understanding as to exactly what it means and how to safely engage in these activities. Light bondage or restraining can add a thrilling new dimension to your sex life. Many people find it highly arousing, since it provides an opportunity to both play and explore issues of power and domination. Some couples report renewed interest in sexual activity as they discover novel visual and physical sensations.

It is essential to set rules prior to this kind of play. Both partners should be equal and willing participants. They should agree together on issues such as what, where, how and how much restraint to use. Safety is always a primary concern, to insure that nobody gets hurt. Having a signal to stop the action is vital for the physical and emotional safety of the partners. This can be done with a word, a phrase, a hand sign or anything else both agree upon that would not spontaneously occur as a result of the sexual activity. You may want to use words such as "onion" or "umbrella", as these are not words typically uttered during sex. Remember this is meant to be fun and not scary or intimidating.

C P R:

Be clear that you both agree you want to try playing in this manner. Then set the rules, keeping in mind that trusting your partner is a vital element in restraining and in most forms of sexual behavior. Start with simple and very safe activities. Restraining your lover can be done with the eyes open and the mouth free to talk. Gently tie a soft scarf around your partner's wrists. As you do this be sure to ask your partner how it feels. The scarf should be tight enough to stay on and give a sense of being tied up, but lose enough so that blood can flow freely and not cause bruising. The scarf should also be loose enough so that the restrained partner can untie it themselves if they so chose. Once the scarf is properly in place you can play! Another element to add is to explore some loving tickling or teasing, pretending that one is at the complete mercy of the other. With this technique, the person who is restrained is often able to sexually abandon themselves more fully than ever before. After all, their hands are immobilized and so nothing is expected of them but to receive pleasure.

Remember that, despite common belief, the one who is restrained is really the one who is in charge. That person always has the power to stop the play if they want to. If you both decide you like this kind of play, you can move on to explore other forms of bondage and domination, such as handcuffs, gags, blindfolds, spanking or whipping. But remember to be safe. For example, never leave the bound person alone in the house. Set the rules in advance and stick to them!

C

P

R

CONTRACEPTION

Sometimes the issue of birth control can cause strain on a relationship. Partners may feel uncared for if they carry the full burden of dealing with contraception. Frequently the fear of pregnancy and/or STDs (sexually transmitted diseases) and STIs (sexually transmitted infections) keep people from enjoying sexual contact and may lead to an avoidance of it all together.

Power struggles with this issue are abundant. For example, men frequently refuse to wear a condom or get a vasectomy. Some women refuse to use any birth control method because they feel contraception is the man's responsibility. These power struggles further complicate the situation and increase the sense of distance in the relationship.

C P R:

Try making the use of barriers (condoms and diaphragms) a fun part of your sexual contact. Men frequently find it erotic to have their partner put the condom on for them. Some women enjoy watching their partners help them prepare and insert their diaphragm. If your partner is taking birth control pills, bring her pill to her with a cup of juice in the morning or remind her to take it before going to bed. You may also want to take turns alternating who will be responsible for contraception at each sexual encounter.

C

P

R

CONCEPTION AND PREGNANCY

Many couples trying to conceive find sex burdensome. Planning for sex to happen during the days of ovulation can turn sex into a chore. Moreover, suggestions from well-meaning friends and family combined with sadness from failed attempts can turn sex into an unpleasant obligation leading to marital tension and even performance anxiety.

If conception is successful and the belly begins to grow, some men are turned off by it, while others find that a pregnant belly is sexy. Watching the woman's belly grow and knowing that the child is his may even increase the man's desire for sex. Similar feelings of increased arousal may occur for the woman as a result of hormonal changes that occur during pregnancy.

As delivery approaches, many women find sex difficult and have little interest in it. While men can usually understand the medical need to stop intercourse in the last part of pregnancy and the weeks after childbirth, they may nevertheless find this interruption of intercourse sexually frustrating and distancing. They sometimes stop holding and kissing the woman altogether so as not to get aroused. As a result, the expectant mother may feel undesirable and rejected.

C P R:

If you are working hard to conceive, be sure to throw in some romance along the way. Remind yourselves that the whole reason for conceiving is that you love each other and want to express and expand that love. For a while, drop all the medical methods you are using to try to conceive and simply make love with each other. This will help balance out the stress and will help minimize the odds that sex will be seen as a chore, even once you have conceived. If some of the methods involve such things as shots and in vitro techniques, be sure to share the experience every step of the way. For example, while producing a sperm sample for the laboratory, bring your partner into the depository room with you to help you produce the sample. If your partner has to give herself hormone shots, be by her side or even learn how to administer the shots to her yourself.

During pregnancy, have sex! Pregnancy can be an extremely sexy time for the woman. She doesn't have to deal with contraception or with worries about getting pregnant so she can be more relaxed with sex. Also, during pregnancy, there is increased blood volume in the woman's pelvic area. This creates engorgement (swelling) that facilitates arousal and orgasm.

Contrary to popular belief, sex will not harm the fetus. Remember that the fetus grows inside the uterus, not inside the vagina. For most, it is only in the very late stages of pregnancy that the penis hitting the cervix may cause a miscarriage, and even that is rare.

Of course, extremely rough play is ill-advised during pregnancy.

This is a good time to remember that sex is not just intercourse. There are a multitude of sexual activities in which you can safely engage while pregnant. For example, manual or oral stimulation is perfectly fine. Touching or licking the clitoris, labia and vulva, or putting a finger in the vagina will cause no harm. And of course, it will not harm the fetus if the woman performs oral sex on the man or manually stimulates his penis. If intercourse is desired, you can explore positions that feel comfortable and won't add stress to the fetus.

For example, rear entry in the spooning position is very safe.

COMPENSATE FOR PHYSICAL PROBLEMS

Physical ailments, disabilities and illnesses certainly can easily lead to a lack of desire. Just look at what happens when we have a bad cold, toothache or headache. Few of us feel sexual when we are in physical distress. Fortunately, our symptoms soon pass and we return to our former sexual frequency and pattern.

If you have a chronic physical condition, however, the same old approaches to sex often won't work. When you are in constant pain and are distracted by bothersome physical symptoms, some compensation is required to make sex work. In an extreme example, one can move from "perfect" physical health to quadriplegia (possibly due to an accident). In this case, major compensation is required. The newly injured person will need to learn ways to find pleasure in the little physical sensations they do have, perhaps only on the face, neck and head. They will also need to learn how to please their partner with the limited capacities left to them. It is said that as long as a person can speak and has use of their eyes and tongue, they still can be a fantastic lover. Of course, less severe physical limitations also require some creative compensation that can lead to great results.

C P R:

If your physical problem involves back, neck, or hip pain, try using lots of oversized pillows. Turn on your side and prop yourself into a comfortable position. Your partner can help by moving the pillows around until you are as comfortable as possible. Experiment with different positions for different kinds of sexual activities. For example, intercourse may be very successful for you in the spoon position, especially with the legs in a scissor position or sitting position. Oral sex may be accomplished by having you find a comfortable position on your back, with your neck supported by a pillow and your partner squatting above you.

You may compensate for physical problems with erections by using a penis constrictor (cock-ring), an erection vacuum pump, or a medication such as Viagra, Levitra or Cialis,

A dry vagina is easily compensated for by use of a personal vaginal lubricant that you can buy either at a pharmacy, adult bookstore or online through an adult enhancement site.

Also, pay attention to your prime time for sex. Perhaps an hour after you've taken your pain medication would work better for you than other times.

Regardless of the physical limitation, never stop being sensual and loving. Also, giving up on your usual script on the manner and order in which you have typically believed sex should occur can help significantly. In some cases, you may also have to forego orgasm and find your pleasure in pleasing your partner, and by the physical and emotional closeness that accompanies this.

Compensate for desire discrepancy

Discrepancy in sexual desire (libido) is the most common sexual difficulty that people face in a relationship. This is not surprising, because it is rare for both partners to want exactly the same sexual activities, at exactly the same time and with exactly the same frequency and intensity. Many couples fight bitterly over this issue.

Most partners differ in their desire for sex. Contrary to popular mythology, where it is always the woman who says, "Not tonight honey. I have a headache," high libido and low libido are not the domain of only one gender. They can occur in both men and women. When desire discrepancies exist in a relationship, the partner with the stronger desire for sex often feels rejected, cheated and resentful - seeing their partner as sexually cold and withholding. The partner with less desire, on the other hand, generally feels pressured and not "normal." They tend to see the more highly sexed partner as always horny, demanding and perverted. They view them as being obsessed with sex – thinking of and wanting nothing but sex, or, what is commonly referred to today as being a "sex addict."

What they are doing is passing a judgment that says, "If you don't hunger for sex with the same frequency that I do, then there is something wrong with you." Wrong? Different is not wrong; it is just not feeling the same as somebody else. Very few of us get hungry for dinner at the exact time and for the exact meal that our partner wants, and yet we don't see our partner as deficient or abnormal. Most of us do not say to our partner, "It's seven p.m. and you're not hungry? What's wrong with you?"" But when our partner has a lower appetite or hunger for sex than we do, many of us tend to see this as a negative comment on our desirability or our skill as a lover. We may also feel that if our partner really loved us that they would always be willing to engage in sex with us. Our partner, on their part, may feel sexually inadequate and guilty that they are depriving us. With these feelings present, sexual activity, when it does occur, may be filled with resentment and pain.

C P R:

This is a good area for compromise. First, verbally acknowledge to each other that you understand that having exactly the same desire for sex is uncommon and unreasonable.

Then determine what each of you see as the preferred frequency for intercourse and find a frequency that is in the middle. The partner with the higher libido will compromise for less sex and the one with the lower libido will compromise for more.

You can introduce compromise in activities as well. If the partner with the lower libido just can't see themselves having intercourse at the agreed-upon frequency, perhaps they could find a compromise behavior. For example, they might assist their partner to orgasm manually, orally or mechanically, while their partner strokes their hair, gives them a foot rub or performs some other sensuous activity. The idea here is to be intimate with each other as often as possible, in whatever form works best for both partners.

If one partner has absolutely no desire for sex at any time, we would suggest a medical checkup and sex therapy as low sex drive may be the result of taking certain medications, or may stem from psychological or behavioral issues such as poor body image or lack of being made love to in a way that pleases us. Also, both low and high libido may be a form of punishing a partner by demanding sex or withholding sex.

COMPENSATE FOR ERECTION PROBLEMS

Despite myth and common belief, men are not always able to obtain and maintain an erection. Most men, even young ones, go through times in their lives when they are unable to achieve or sustain erections. Society is starting to clearly understand this reality, as evidenced by the many advertisements currently running on TV and in magazines for Viagra, Levitra and Cialis, pharmaceuticals aimed at solving "ED" – Erectile Dysfunction. The desire for these magical pills was so intense when they first appeared on the market that certain men were willing to pay fifty dollars a pill!

ED is more commonly known as impotence. This term is losing favor, as it falsely indicates that a man has no power, especially when it comes to sex. Sadly, many men still believe that today. They have such a great emotional investment in getting an erection that when it doesn't happen at the right moment, they label themselves unmanly and worthless in the bedroom. They often shy away from sex so as not to have to deal with their "shameful" situation, even when their partner protests that it doesn't matter.

Sometimes the ED is due to a medical problem such as diabetes, high blood pressure, arteriosclerosis, poor circulation or low testosterone levels. It can also be the result of taking certain medications, including anti-depressants, heart medications, blood pressure medications and sleeping pills, or it may be the aftermath of an operation such as prostate surgery. In these medically induced cases, medications like Viagra may make a big difference and be all it takes to resolve this problem. There are times when ED is caused by medical problems, and yet, medication cannot always resolve the problem. In fact, many blood pressure and heart medications and antidepressants have side effects that inhibit erections.

In a great many instances, however, ED can also have a psychological cause such as stress, exhaustion, nervousness, anger, or performance anxiety. When ED is not due to a medical problem, taking such medications may be counterproductive. No matter what the cause, there are things one can do to overcome ED or successfully cope with it, in addition to, or instead of, pharmaceutical intervention.

C P R:

For the Man:

Provided that you are capable of achieving erections on your own, practice getting and maintaining them. Stimulate the penis until it gets hard. If you have difficulty, introduce fantasy or pornography to help you get or stay aroused. You might also try a penis constrictor (cock ring) to help you maintain firmness. Once you have an erection, aim to keep it alive rather than ejaculating. Slow down your strokes while still maintaining firmness. Try to make the erection last at least 10 minutes. Practice this CPR at least three times a week until your erections become more dependable.

For the Couple:

Ask your partner to assist you in getting an erection and then slowing down the movement to help you keep the erection for at least 10 minutes without ejaculating. Let your partner know when you need slower, lighter, faster or heavier strokes.

*If you are the partner of a man with erection problems, you may wonder why you should be involved in the solution. The answer is that **if one partner in a relationship has a sexual problem, then the relationship has a sexual problem**. By lovingly participating in the suggested CPRs, you are doing your part to heal the sexual relationship.*

If you are an older man, you may need to compensate by changing some of your earlier habits or expectations. Most men do not lose the ability to achieve erections with age. Instead, the erections are usually not as firm and take longer to achieve. Allow extra time for kissing and touching so that you can get as aroused as possible before your partner stimulates your penis.

Even when a penis is flaccid (not erect, soft), it can still be used for sexual activity. Rub the non-erect penis against your partner's genitals, anus, or nipples, between their thighs or breasts, or in your partner's mouth. Many also enjoy stuffing the soft penis into the vagina or anus and using fingers to keep it in place. The penis often gets firm once it is inside.

By pleasuring your partner with manual and/or oral stimulation, or by using a vibrator, we hope that you will learn to abandon the false belief that you must have an erection to be a good lover. Erections frequently come and stay when the perceived pressure to have them is removed.

RAPID (PREMATURE) EJACULATION

Rapid ejaculation is a common reason that couples seek a sex therapist. Couples are quite often disappointed, frustrated and, sometimes, very angry when a man ejaculates quicker than he and his partner want him to. In addition to intercourse being cut short, curtailing much pleasure for both, the man is frequently left with a feeling of inadequacy. Pornography and cultural myths lead men to believe that to be a good lover they must "last" all night. In actuality, the average length of time for intercourse is less than five minutes.

His partner's negative feelings about the rapid ejaculation frequently add to the incredible loss of self-esteem the man may experience. Couples often have failures trying different methods to solve it and, as a result, frequently give up on sex altogether.

Men learn ineffective methods for solving this problem from friends, family and the media. These so-called cures usually involve some kind of mind game in which the man is encouraged to think of non-sexually arousing things, such as sports or a mother-in-law. While this sometimes leads to a lack of ejaculation, it also typically results in a loss of pleasure and perhaps, a loss of erection altogether.

Then there are creams and lubricated condoms available to numb the penis in an effort decrease the sensitivity, therefore delaying ejaculation. Unsubstantiated herbal remedies available on the market claim to act similarly. However, both these methods also decrease enjoyment and do not carry over to times when they are unavailable for the man to use.

In addition, some medical doctors even prescribe anti-depressants and/or anti-anxiety medications to help men reduce their excitement, therefore allegedly helping them control their ejaculation.

C P R:

C
P
R

Ejaculation control is a learned skill, much like that of controlling one's bladder (holding one's urine). Almost all men can learn to do it. The easiest and most successful method is the "stop-start" approach. The best way to learn and apply this method is to first try it alone, while masturbating, and then introduce partner contact until the desired results are achieved.

During masturbation, rub the penis with a dry hand until ejaculation is very close, or just before what is called the "point of ejaculatory inevitability." Then stop. Wait until the sensation of ejaculatory inevitably diminishes – a few seconds to a couple of minutes – and then continue to masturbate. Do this at least three times before allowing yourself to ejaculate.

As you gain a sense of control, slowly introduce greater sensation by speeding up your strokes and by adding moisture, such as a lubricant or lotion. This produces a closer feeling to what it is like to have one's penis inside a vagina, mouth or anus. Repeat the three stops before ejaculating with each new stimulation and wait until you're satisfied with the results before proceeding to the next step.

After control is gained with your own hand, move on to partner contact. Be sure to start this CPR by having your partner stroke your penis with a dry hand. Move on to a moist hand when ready.

Finally, introduce oral sex or intercourse. When control seems to be good, simply stopping any sucking or thrusting, waiting a few moments and then proceeding, can produce the desired results.

PENETRATION VS. CONTAINMENT

Penetration and thrusting are what most people think of when they say "sex" or "real sex." This is a reference to a penis penetrating or entering a vagina or an anus, and thrusting in and out. This sexual activity usually ends when the man ejaculates. In this model of intercourse, the penis is active and the vagina or anus is passive. The man whose penis is thrusting dictates the speed and force and usually feels in charge. Meanwhile, the partner is either enjoying what is being done to them or, at least, putting up with it.

Containment refers to a very similar process in which the penis is put into the vagina or anus. However, it is the person whose vagina or anus is penetrated who is in charge of any movement and pressure. The man whose penis is inside is the passive one.

New sensations and emotional responses may be experienced by using this model of intercourse. For example, the once-passive partner may have previously experienced a sense of being "used" during penetration. Now, in the active role, this partner can feel like an equal, one who shares or controls the activity. By being in charge of any movement, they may now discover parts of their vagina or anus that enjoy stimulation – parts they were unaware of when being passive. Similarly, the once active, but now passive, partner may find great pleasure by exerting less energy and may also enjoy new sensations that thrusting did not allow.

Many men find that they are able to last longer (refrain longer from ejaculating) and enjoy themselves more by taking this passive role. Many women find that they are better able to achieve orgasm in the more active role. Gay men who were in the passive role and are now in the active role report finding much greater pleasure.

How to Breathe Life into a Dead, Dying or Dull Sex Life

C P R:

Agree in advance of any physical contact that you will try the containment approach. Proceed with romance and initial sexual contact in your usual manner. When you are both sufficiently aroused, insert the penis into a lubricated vagina or anus. You may assume any sexual position you like, such as missionary, sitting, or doggy style. Some thrusting is important at this point so that full insertion occurs without losing the erection. Then keep the penis still. If you are the one who is containing the penis inside you, imagine you are giving the penis a massage. Squeeze the penis and relax. Squeeze and relax. Move around to discover different levels of sensation and the position that feels just right. If you're the one whose penis is being contained, be sure to occasionally move so that the penis feels enough stimulation to remain erect. Try this several times as it sometimes takes a while to find the right muscles to create pleasure. Be patient, as it may take some time and practice until you both feel the full sensations.

Write down at least three ways in which you found containment different than penetration and discuss them with each other:

1._____

2._____

3._____

PORNOGRAPHY

While pornography may be highly entertaining to some of us, and even helps stimulate sexual desire, it is a poor teacher of real sex. Pornography can create unrealistic physical and sexual expectations of both ourselves and of our partners because it sends false messages such as: all women have fantastically fit bodies; are exhibitionists; are easily orgasmic; are always willing to please their partner with any kind of sexual activity (with little or no building up of desire, with no effort to prepare the woman's body properly for intercourse) and no attention to her own orgasm. Men are equally falsely depicted as having an erection on demand; having enormous penises; being able to engage in intercourse for hours at a time, and being able to ejaculate several times within as little as twenty minutes. These depictions frequently leave us feeling inadequate and with unrealistic expectations of our own bodies, sexual functioning and response and those of our partner.

C P R:

C
P
R

Talk with each other about the false nature of lovemaking depicted in pornography. Acknowledge the fact that the people in the films are actors and actresses getting paid to put on a show. They are given carefully chosen wardrobe and have make-up artists who prepare them, sometimes for hours in advance; and it takes many hours of filming and editing to put together what appear to be only minutes in the final product. Furthermore, remind each other that almost all pornography is made for a heterosexual man's fantasy.

If you choose to watch pornography together, consider finding films that are made to fit your taste. For example, there are film companies that produce pornography made by and designed for women. These films typically take the graphic activities that most straight men prefer and mix in a plot and sensuous background that women may like. Many films made for gay men are excellent in depicting what gay men actually do with each other, and explore real issues between male lovers, such as love and the need for gentle touch. The same is typically true for films made by and for lesbian couples.

If you chose to view pornography together, discuss what is depicted in the films. Write down three things you viewed that you both would like to try.

1. _____

2. _____

3. _____

Now write down anything you viewed that you don't want to try, and discuss why.

1. _____

2. _____

3. _____

REVIEW

Reviewing helps people look at where they've been, what their life was like when they started a journey, and how they have grown through it. Fond and painful memories may arise. As you reach the end of this book, it's important that you review your progress, and your journey through it.

C P R:

Answer the following questions and discuss together how your relationship was when you first picked up CPR for Your Sex Life.

- *Was your sex life in trouble?* _____

- *Did you view your partner with disinterest? Anger?* _____

- *Were you bored and disenchanted with each other?* _____

- *What do you think would have happened if you had not read and worked with this book? Would your sex life be dying now? Dead?* _____

- *Take another look at the first chapter. Were you the ones we were referring to when we discussed a loss of interest in each other? Were you able to relate to some of the pain?*
  _____

- *Look at the checkup and the checklist. Do you remember them bringing up pain?*
  _____

- *Were you able to discuss this with your partner at the time?* _____

- *Now thumb through the Cs, Ps and Rs. Were any of them more significant than the others in helping you?* _____

What did you learn about your partner?

_____

_____

_____

What did your partner learn about you?

_____

_____

_____

What did you really like that was not part of your sex life or intimacy prior to reading this book?

_____

_____

_____

What CPR's did you skip or shy away from? Why?

_____

_____

_____

Were the goals you stated during your checkup fulfilled? What would you say contributed to their fulfillment or lack of it?

C

P

R

_____

_____

_____

_____

Review your progress together. See if you both agree on the state of your sex life today. Do you need or want to go back and review parts of the book? Doing so occasionally will be helpful down the road as a refresher or booster shot for your sex life

NOTES:

_____

_____

_____

_____

_____

_____

_____

_____

_____

_____

Conclusion

Congratulations! You did it! You completed your CPR journey!

We wrote *CPR for your Sex Life* to help breathe life into the dead, dying or dull sex lives of couples who love each other and are committed to each other and the relationship. We emphasized that "life", with all its challenges and stressors can easily get in the way of a quality sex life. The demands of work and family life exhaust most couples, and as a result, sex goes on the back burner. Our aim was to help make intimacy – both emotional and sexual – a priority again.

By using a workbook method, we encouraged you to discover your own needs and your own recipes for re-establishing a vital sex life. We also suggested that you and your partner together engage in what is typically considered courtship behavior. Our hope was that you would become more loving, romantic, respectful and considerate to each other and that these behaviors would be the stepping stones to passion and great sex.

We stressed that if you diligently worked through this book, you would have a much better relationship and sex life than when you first began reading it. We hope that has occured for you and your partner and that the CPR method has brought new life, excitement and joy into your relationship.

Your focus now should be on integrating your newfound relationship skills into your daily life and maintaining them throughout your lifetime. It is easy to lose gains if we aren't constantly vigilant. Relapse is to be expected. Should this occur in your relationship, we suggest that you go back and revisit the CPRs that have the most meaning to you – those that feel like they will best address the relapse issues. For most couples who have completed this CPR workbook, this should be sufficient to get you back on track. If that is not the case for you, consider seeking out professional help with a qualified sex therapist. Make sure you bring *CPR for Your Sex Life* with you so that the therapist knows what you have tried. They may very well recommend that you continue to work with this book, along with their personal support, as they help guide you past the hurdles that keep you from reaching your desired goals.

Long-term loving relationships require nurturing, sowing new seeds of love and revisiting what has worked in the past. The same holds true when it comes to having a satisfying intimate and sexual life with our partners. So periodically review this workbook in the future – not just when you're having problems, but also when things are going well. And, by all means, don't forget to celebrate your love!

We wish you well and hope that you will have a life filled with incredible love and great sex!

Mildred & Stephen

References

1. Bailey, Daniel, *The Nature of Prostitution – Sorry, No Kissing: My Encounters with Professional Escorts*, Authorhouse Books, Bloomington, IN, 2004

2. Masters, W. and Johnson, V., *Human Sexual Inadequacy*, Boston, Little, Brown, 1970

3. Montagu, Ashley, *Touching: The Human Significance of the Skin*, New York, Harper-Collins, 1986

4. Phillips, Debora with Judd, Robert, *Sexual Confidence*, Boston, Bantam Books, 1982

5. Work: An Australian Study 10/13/04, www.sexwork.com

About the Authors

Mildred L. Brown holds a doctorate degree in human sexuality. She is a Clinical Sexologist, a Board Certified Sex Therapist and a Diplomate of Sex Therapy who is in private practice in Laguna Woods, California. She specializes in sex therapy and gender identity issues. She is also a Professor of Clinical Sexology and a Sex Therapy Clinical Supervisor at the Institute for Advanced Study of Human Sexuality in San Francisco. For many years, she has also run marriage encounter weekends for couples. Dr. Brown's groundbreaking book, *True Selves: Understanding Transsexualism for Families, Friends, Coworkers and Helping Professionals*, co-authored with Chloe Rounsley, published in 1996, has become a classic in the field of gender identity.

Stephen L. Braveman is a Licensed Marriage and Family Therapist, a Certified Diplomate of Sex Therapy, a Gender Specialist and a Tantra Educator with a private practice in Monterey, California. He is also a current leader in the field of sex therapy, serving on the Board of Directors for AASECT – American Association of Sexuality Educators, Counselors and Therapists – and is a AASECT Certified Clinical Supervisor. Stephen served as President of the California Association of Marriage and Family Therapists – Monterey County, has taught in many Graduate Psychology programs and is the author of *"Innovative Methods of Treating Patients with Sexual Trauma"* in *Innovations in Clinical Practice: Focus on Sexual Health, 2007*. He is also a regular contributor to many websites, journals, magazines and newspapers, and makes frequent appearances on TV and radio.